BEYOND PROFIT & PRODUCTIVITY

Putting Positive Workplace Culture to Work

Paul Krismer
Jackson Kerchis

©Copyright 2024 Paul Krismer and Jackson Kerchis
Beyond Profit & Productivity
Putting Positive Workplace Culture to Work

All rights reserved. No part of this book can be reproduced without the written permission of the authors.

eBook ISBN: 978-1-962570-59-6
Paperback ISBN: 978-1-962570-60-2
Hardcover ISBN: 978-1-962570-61-9
Ingram Spark ISBN: 978-1-962570-62-6
Library of Congress Control Number: 2024906824
Printed in the United States of America

Design: Marigold2k
Cover Creation: Angie Ayala
Interior Design: Marigold2k
Publisher: Spotlight Publishing House –
https://spotlightpublishinghouse.com

Contact:
Website: www.HappinessMeansBusiness.com

BEYOND PROFIT & PRODUCTIVITY

Putting Positive Workplace Culture to Work

Paul Krismer
Jackson Kerchis

Goodyear, Arizona

Contents

Introduction vii

Part I — THE BUSINESS CASE FOR BETTING ON
        HAPPINESS 1
Chapter 1:   Happy People → Successful People.........................3
Chapter 2:   From Individuals to Organizations 9
Chapter 3:   Happiness Means Business......................................15
Chapter 4:   The Unfortunate Truth of Negativity Bias 25
Chapter 5:   Who Dictates Your Culture? Why
                Supervisors and Managers Matter 29

Part II — BEYOND MOTIVATION: TOWARD AN
        ENERGIZED WORKFORCE...................................35
Chapter 6:   An Office as a Metaphor for Organizational
                Psychology..37
Chapter 7:   THE LOBBY Meeting Basic Needs........................45
Chapter 8:   The Fire Escape Meeting Perceived Must-haves 51
Chapter 9:   Lunchroom Belonging and Connecting
                with Groups 57
Chapter 10: Conference Hall Self-esteem and Knowing
                One's Own Value...65
Chapter 11: Executive Offices Self-Actualization One of
                Two: Autonomy...73
Chapter 12: Rooftop Self-Actualization Two of Two—
                Meaning 81
Chapter 13: Lightning Rod Cultivating Positive Energy.............89

Part III — ENGINEERING WORKPLACE
    CULTURE: THEORY TO ACTION 99
Chapter 14: Designing Cultural Rhythm and Accountability....101
Chapter 15: Establishing Baseline Measures 109
Chapter 16: Positive Paradigm 117
Chapter 17: Appreciative Inquiry 125
Chapter 18: Creating Positive Emotional Context: Five
    Best Practices 135
Chapter 19: Emotional Intelligence...145
Chapter 20: Whole-Brain Leadership 153
Chapter 21: Running Toward Attitude Problems.......................161
Chapter 22: Invest in Coaching...169
Chapter 23: Rethinking Performance Evaluation.......................177
Chapter 24: A Direct Line to the Ultimate Purpose...................185

Conclusion: Beyond Profit and Productivity:
    A Happier World..189

Introduction

Have you ever thought "work sucks"?

Have you ever worked with colleagues who were just putting in time?

Have you seen office politics lead to foolish contests between competing egos?

Have you seen bureaucracy and complex processes stifle creativity and entrepreneurialism?

Have you seen good people quit and the "wrong" people stay?

If any of these resonate with you, then you're reading the right book at the right time.

Anyone who has spent more than a few weeks in nearly any large business has seen and felt weak workplace culture. A lucky few will work in organizations that consistently burst with positive, contagious energy and commitment. The rest of us, unfortunately, know what it's like to be in a place where negative, stressed-out colleagues contemplate leaving. Or, even worse, we know co-workers who are so discouraged that they've given up *and stay* with no real commitment to the business. They bring a special poison, where their disengagement wreaks havoc on the motivation of everyone around them.

You intuitively know poor morale cripples a business. People sit quietly in meetings. They go through the motions of getting stuff done, but their genuine enthusiasm is absent. Entire armies of staff either have too little to do, or far too much. Millions of employees work productively for half days, stretched painfully over eight-hour

INTRODUCTION

periods. Conversely, other untold millions face so many pressures that they work ten hours days consistently and never feel caught up or that they've done their work in a fashion that instills deep pride.

Almost everyone has had a boss with terrible leadership skills—sometimes a bully and other times, someone so weak that obvious and frequent problems go unaddressed.

Some of you reading this will have experiences with open warfare between labor and management. Disrespectful to-your-face dialogue is common.

Tragically, modern large workplaces too often feel soul-sucking… joyful learning never happens… enthusiastic teamwork and playful innovation are gone… labor is bought, but hearts are on strike. These places have massive competitive *disadvantages*. They lose productivity and profitability. They have poor customer service, lots of absenteeism, and are followers, playing catch-up to the companies that truly innovate. These businesses are where the "get up and go!" got up and left a long time ago.

In some workplaces, the cancer of poor culture may not have metastasized through the organization, but the tumors are present in pockets… threatening the body… the very life of the organization.

This is my space. I've spent over thirty years of my life looking at, studying, and developing tools to ignite organizations on a path toward flourishing workplace cultures. I've served in executive roles in very large organizations throughout most of that time. Since 2016, I've dedicated my business to fixing the problems that lead to workforce decline. I've consulted many hundreds of different businesses, in different industries—everything from fishing to banking, to hospitals to pulp mills, and the US military. I've logged hundreds of hours as an Executive Coach. Our mission at Happiness Means Business is to help 1,000,000 professionals and 100,000 soldiers be happier at work because Happiness is the greatest gift we can give to ourselves, to the world, and to future generations.

The work I do has many formats. I speak at conferences and corporate events all over the world. I train leadership teams, including frontline supervisors. I consult with HR teams. I coach individual leaders. Everything I do has one aim—creating leaders equipped to build and sustain great workplace cultures.

I designed this book to put a lifetime of accumulated expertise into 150 or so pages. This book teaches theory about what makes humans tick, both individually and in groups. It comes loaded with practical, actionable strategies you can use to make a difference in the businesses and teams you lead immediately.

Workplace culture is the key to exceptional success as an organization. In fact, culture is every bit as important as strategic vision and customer value proposition. This book provides a road map to optimal culture. It tells you how to create one that sets your organization apart.

At the time of this writing (late 2022), there's an incredibly tight labor market, resulting in record-low unemployment and massive churn in the workforce. The popular press is calling this period "The Great Resignation." Droves of workers are leaving their organizations looking for something better. What is better? The press rarely articulates it succinctly, but put simply, people want to be happier at work.

In this book, you'll see the word "happiness" a fair bit. When I use this word, read it as an umbrella term for a contextual dimension of workforce well-being, positive leadership, organizational psychology, and culture. This amounts to an entire *dimension* of business that's often overlooked.

Even for leaders who acknowledge the role of happiness and culture in business, there's a temptation to not take it seriously enough. Culture is nice, but surely it can't be as important as the "hard stuff," like financials, operations, and distribution.

INTRODUCTION

But, as you'll learn in this book, workforce well-being, culture, and worker engagement are inseparable from these other more traditional business concerns. Happiness means creativity, productivity, effectiveness, and profitability. Happiness means business.

With some subtlety, this book is also a wake-up call. Can our businesses step past short-term quarterly profits and see a grander vision? Can business be a force for good, not only for the people in their workforces, but for the world? Can happiness and well-being be the vision that propels organizations to greatness? My challenge for you is to see the "yes" to all three questions in the pages to come.

How to Use This Book

Part One discusses the business case for investing in your workplace culture.

Part Two covers employee psychology within an organization. It provides a theoretical underpinning to understanding a workforce's emotional and developmental needs.

Part Three is a practical method to get started. I've provided measurable, tested interventions you can build on.

The book is deliberately concise.

You're busy. My respect for your time motivates this format. However, do not mistake this stylistic choice as "light" reading. The content of this book could easily be the primary aim of an entire, ambitious career.

A relentlessly energized, high performance work culture is magic—few organizations have it. Those that do are unstoppable. They have specific attributes that make all the difference.

Each chapter has a key takeaway. If you've thoroughly engaged with a chapter, you will finish with at least one, if not a handful, of next actions. Each chapter ends with an opportunity for you to reflect and plan your implementation.

Learning is of no value if it doesn't stir you into action. "If you let your learning lead to knowledge, you become a fool. If you let your learning lead to action, you become wealthy," as famous entrepreneur Jim Rohn said.

If you read this book as a leader with a genuine desire to serve the people you lead, then you'll also use this as a workbook. Using the provided space for your reflections and action planning, you'll have a drafted action plan for a massive culture change after the last chapter.

Two small qualifications before we get started:

1) Humans are diverse. There are superficial differences, like skin color; and there are deep differences born out of culture, education, social conditioning, and more. This book deliberately speaks in relevant generalizations. What I share about human psychology is almost always true for nearly every individual. We're alike in our basic motivations. I won't waste your time writing about the exceptions. So, I'll say it just once now: some small proportion of individuals vary from the norm.

2) We are two writers. Wise editors said it would serve you, the reader, if we wrote the book as one voice. So, we've written this book's perspective as though it were mine: Paul Krismer. I am the lead author. Jackson Kerchis, my talented co-author, has his brilliance reflected in every page of the book. He's an expert business consultant with a unique perspective at the intersection of happiness and

INTRODUCTION

business. His depth of experience, profound insights, and firm foundation in the science of happiness have massively contributed to this work. If you like what you read here, it's every bit to Jackson's credit as to mine.

If you're ready for the tools to improve your business and create happiness at work, let's get started!

PART I

THE BUSINESS CASE FOR BETTING ON HAPPINESS

Chapter 1

Happy People →
Successful People

I was so excited when, at seven-years-old, a large delivery truck showed up at my house with a new living room set. Tables, chairs, a couch—the whole shebang!

I couldn't have cared less about the furniture itself. It was the packaging that excited me. My mom would give me all the cardboard containers each piece of furniture was being delivered in. Along with some old sheets of weather-worn plywood, I was certain I had the foundation for an amazing backyard fort.

I had two best friends in the neighborhood: Dale and Stephen. The day after the furniture delivery, we set out to build the most amazing fort to protect us from all manner of girl and parent invasions. We'd live big—wild—in our own land, with our own home base!

We toiled for hours and hours. There were debates, of course, but they were punctuated with enthusiasm and commitment. We got so much done. Our focus was complete. My mom left food nearby so we wouldn't have to break from our passionate work. It was a rush of camaraderie and productivity.

Can you feel that energy? The enthusiasm? It was pure joy. It was play at its best.

And hopefully, maybe you too, have felt this same way in precious moments at work. Perhaps, unlike a seven-year-old, you were grounded more in reality than in forts to keep imaginary invaders away. But like a seven-year-old, you found yourself fully immersed in a task. You thoroughly enjoyed the real companionship of colleagues, as you collectively made something that brought meaning to you, individually and as a contribution to both your business and the people your business serves. It was fun, wasn't it? It made you happy!

Happiness leads to success. It's a fact that when a person has an abundance of positive emotions, they get better life outcomes.

A landmark meta-study[1]—that is, a study of studies—shows that regardless of which measure of life success you inquire about, happy people achieve more.

With well over two hundred independent, peer-reviewed, published papers involving over 275,000 human participants, the consensus is clear: happiness fuels success.

I don't say this as a feel-good sentiment.

The following observations are true.

When a person has an abundance of positive emotions,

a) Career progression and income are predictably better.
b) Health is more robust, including boosted immune response, better cardiovascular functioning, and a longer life.
c) Relationships are characterized by warmth and persistence; marriages are more likely to succeed.
d) Cognitively, people perform better across different measures of intelligence, including logical problem solving, creativity, and access to memory.
e) Bizarrely, peripheral vision is more expansive—happy people literally see more.
f) Energy, as a measure of sustained task focus and perseverance is improved.

---

[1] Lyuobomisrky, King, Deiner. The benefits of frequent positive affect: does happiness lead to success? Psychol Bull. 2005 Nov,131(6): 803-55. Doi: 10.1037/0033-2909.131.6.803. PMID: 16351326.

This list could go on and on. Proven, real benefits of happiness are known.

What does it mean to be happy? Is it simply a wide grin and an irrepressible desire to skip, dance, and sing? No. This depiction of "happiness" reduces it to something frivolous and often contextually inappropriate.

Instead, we should see happiness as an umbrella term referring to any of the many well researched positive emotions.[2] These emotions are all "happy" ones:

- joy
- gratitude
- interest
- hope
- pride
- inspiration
- serenity
- amusement
- awe
- love

A healthy array of positive emotions leads to good life outcomes.

Can a determined individual who desires to be happier learn skills that reliably, and over the long term, make them happier? And will these happiness skills result in more life success? Yes, and yes.

Research by Sonja Lyubomirsky, Martin Seligman, Ed Diener, and many others, proves that people can learn interventions that lead to increased happiness.

The science of happiness and human flourishing works. And as mentioned above—these happier individuals are more creative,

---

[2] Barbara Fredrickson, Ph.D. in her 2009 book *Positivity*.

engaged, and effective. As author Shawn Achor puts it — "happiness is the precursor to success".

This is consensus science.

If these conclusions about individual human beings are scientifically true, can happiness empower entire groups of people so they can be more successful? Can we use similar interventions aimed at increasing positive emotions within organizations? The answer awaits in the next chapter.

Reflection:

1) How happy are you at this moment? Take a cross culturally, accurate assessment of your personal happiness in just a couple of minutes.
   -This resource is available for free at:
   www.HappinessMeansBusiness.com/BPP
2) Consider your own experience. Are you most effective when you feel good?
3) How do the most successful people in your organization carry themselves?

Key takeaways:

   1)

   2)

   3)

Chapter 2

From Individuals to Organizations

I recall working with a client who was aware that their business had a culture problem yet didn't know where the problem lived or how it got there. Why were people disengaged, grumpy, and leaving at an alarming pace? In my usual way, I asked permission to poke around and do some discovery work. They introduced me to a few frontline supervisors, and I asked to sit in on some meetings. Years later, one meeting still stands out.

A guy named Dave was the "star" new supervisor. Everyone told me so. He was the right guy to be promoted. He knew his department's work exceptionally well. He'd come from the front lines himself. Through many years of diligent work, he learned to troubleshoot the start-up issues customers had with the complex processor his company sold. He was very good at it.

The meeting I attended with Dave was a regular monthly departmental meeting. Dave had an agenda. He started punctually. He was effective at getting through each item. And he invited questions.

Dave's strength was detailed problem-solving. He was great at it. He didn't shy away from technical issues. Dave liked puzzles. And when they promoted him to team supervisor, the only substantial leadership advice he got was to just be himself.

Unfortunately, that was the problem… Dave was a total buzzkill.

He led meetings the same way he analyzed a short circuit on a food processor. Every input was a potential source of the problem.

He liked things, more than people. He spoke about problems, never successes. He was curt and unemotional. His staff didn't hate him, but they got zero positive energy from him. He set the tone, and everyone sang the tune.

Have you been there? Have you sat through meetings with uninspired, negative leaders? Sometimes it's hard to put our finger on why you want to throw yourself out the nearest window, but you know the urge is there!

Dave was one of many subtle contributors to an emotionally depressed workplace culture.

Many meta-studies[3] have been done regarding emotional interventions in workplaces. These meta-studies bring together quality, peer-reviewed studies where academics ran experiments to see if emotional/morale changes followed from deliberate interventions and if said changes resulted in different business outcomes.

Once again, there's a large enough body of work to reach consensus science. Changing collective emotions at work to more positive states drive business improvements.

We can summarize in terms of three components:

1) a positive intervention is implemented, causing,
2) situational changes—measurable observations of different behaviors, resulting in

---

[3] Here are a few references for the interested reader: a) Transformational Leadership and Performance, Kovjanic et.al., Journal of Occupational and Organizational Psychology, 18 June 2013; b) The Added Value of the Positive: A literature review of positive psychology interventions in organizations, Meyers et.al., European Journal of Work and Organizational Psychology, 2013; and c) Meta-Analysis of the Impact of Positive Psychological Capital on Employee Attitudes, Behaviors, and Performance, Avey et.al, Human Resource Development Quarterly, June 2011

3) healthier workforces, improved productivity, and increased profitability.

Let's expand on these three components from a practical business perspective.

One) **Positive Intervention**—to qualify for inclusion in a meta-study, researchers look for peer-reviewed, published studies where a deliberate change to emotional context was sought.

A variety of workplace goals qualify as a "deliberate change to emotional context." Some businesses sought to reduce anger and hostility in the workplace. Others wanted to see job satisfaction scores improve on annual surveys. Still others examined increasing trust among colleagues. Emotional goals varied from less stress, greater frequency of positive feelings, to overall employee engagement. Each of these has an emotional context. Good research shows measurable and desired emotional changes resulting from planned interventions.

So, what happens when the mood of a workplace changes?

Two) **Situational Change**—within the businesses that had an emotional shift, many performance changes were observed. Sometimes the changes were based on the different designs of studies. For example, some researchers only looked for customer service improvements resulting from the emotional change; other researchers were curious to see reduced sick leave usage. We know of broad, demonstrable changes occurring when a workplace has intentional shifts toward more abundant positive emotions.

These changes include:

a) less employee turnover

b) fewer sick days
c) faster recovery from time loss injuries
d) improved safety
e) boosted quality metrics
f) enhanced creativity and innovation
g) more customer satisfaction
h) higher measures of self-reported energy and engagement
i) enhanced interpersonal relationships
j) increased organizational citizenship

While this list of benefits is impressive, I want to explore the last one in more detail: *organizational citizenship*. Academics use this term to mean that individuals *volunteer* more of themselves. That's when people work outside of the bounds of their formal job descriptions. They see the needs in their organization, and they step in to fulfill them. They look for projects and initiatives that advance the mission of their companies. They need much less supervision. They're self-motivated. And they get stuff done even when bureaucracy sets up roadblocks. Businesses that have high levels of organizational citizenship are powerful. They harness the power of a workforce that *believes* in their company.

When high levels of organizational citizenship are present, an employer has moved beyond paying for labor. They've won hearts and minds.

Three) **Bottom-line Results**—There's no surprise here. When deliberate programs to increase positive emotions occur, organizations get healthier, more loyal employees who are more productive. Necessarily, these fortunate businesses become more profitable.

Are you curious how big this bottom-line difference can be? In the next chapter, you can see the tangible, financial impact of improving culture.

Reflection:

1) In what ways do you understand the emotional context of your business? How does it collectively feel at your workplace on an average day?
2) In what ways is there room for improvement?
3) What emotional context do you bring to your workplace?

Key takeaways:

1)

2)

3)

Chapter 3

Happiness Means Business

Happiness means business. That's not just a cute, upbeat catchphrase. Well-being and positivity have real, bottom-line implications for business and organizations. Business leaders who cannot embrace this will go the way of those who failed to embrace automation, innovation, and digital transformation.

This chapter dives into the financial impact of happiness, or unhappiness, on organizations.

More than one past client of mine knew their business was at risk of closure because of massive culture deficits. In several instances, change implemented over periods as little as six months turned things around. It's rare to have everything wrong in a culture. Often, a few strategic interventions make big differences fast. You'll see this as you look at the BIG numbers reflected in this chapter.

Calculating the precise financial implications of organizational well-being and culture is a bit more ambiguous than other calculations. It may be rather easy to model how changes in a commodity price will drive costs through a firm's value chain. But how will managers *feel* more positive change financial performance?

As you think about this, it may be helpful to think in terms of losses and gains. In other words, (1) what is poor culture costing you? And (2) what would improve culture generate for you?

Here are some of the major costs associated with well-being in organizations.

1) *Mental Health*—Mental health challenges are common among workers. According to research from the Harvard Business

Review, 76% of respondents across all organizational levels reported at least one symptom of a mental health condition. What's more, researchers found that C-level and executive workers were *more* likely to report at least one symptom.[4] So it's almost a guarantee that even if your organization is doing well–most employees will struggle with mental health in some capacity. According to an independent review by Deloitte–the average annual cost to employers of poor mental health is approximately $1,560 per employee.[5] Note that figure is calculated across all employees–not just those who reported an illness. They calculated this figure based on data from the EU. Given the substantially greater healthcare costs in the United States, this figure is undoubtedly far larger for U.S. employers. The average Fortune 500 company employs around sixty thousand people. So, with this general barometer–a typical Fortune 500 company loses over $93.6 million per year in mental health costs!

2) *Turnover*–This is one of the most tangible costs of poor culture. According to Kelly Greenwood, founder of Mind Share Partners, 34% of all respondents had left a role for mental health reasons (both voluntarily and involuntarily) at some point.[6] That number jumps to 75% for Gen Zers. Global HR strategist and former Deloitte principal, Josh Bersin, explains that the total cost of losing an employee can range from tens of

---

[4] Kelly Greenwood and Julia Anas "It's a New Era for Mental Health at Work" in the Harvard Business Review.
[5] Deloitte, "Mental health and employers: The case for investment" – A supporting study for the Independent Review.
[6] Kelly Greenwood, Vivek Bapat, and Mike Maughan "Research: People Want Their Employers to Talk About Mental Health" in the Harvard Business Review.

thousands of dollars to 1.5 to 2 times annual salary.[7] The major cost factors embedded within turnover cost include:

a. Recruiting costs to hire a replacement (advertising, interviewing, screening, hiring)
b. Onboarding costs
c. Lost productivity
d. Training costs
e. Cultural impact (e.g., other workers discouraged by loss)

These figures vary widely based on industry, firm size, and region. Some useful figures come from a research report by an online tech community, Built In. Their data suggests turnover costs include $1,500 for hourly employees, 100 to 150% of an employee's salary for technical positions, and up to 213% of an employee's salary for C-suite positions. Think of it this way: when a $400,000 Vice-President leaves for a happier workplace, it costs the company about $850,000!

3) *Absenteeism*—We lose over 200 million workdays because of mental health conditions each year amounting to $16.8 billion in employee productivity lost.[8] Data from the UK shows that at the average workplace, an employee will take 6.3 sick days per year; however, at workplaces listed among the 101 best places to work, this number drops to 2.7. So, moving from average to great could decrease absence by 57%. This has massive financial implications for firms across all industries.

---

[7] Josh Bersin "Employee Retention Now a Big Issue: Why the Tide has Turned" on LinkedIn.
[8] Greenwood, Bapat, and Maughan "Research: People Want Their Employers to Talk About Mental Health."

*4) **Productivity**—*Unhappy workers, even when they do show up, are far less productive than their counterparts. These workers also sap the productive energy from their coworkers. Happier employees are more efficient, more creative, and produce higher quality work. Employee satisfaction even directly affects the consumer. A study shows hospitals with the lowest employee satisfaction had the lowest patient satisfaction, and hospitals with the highest employee satisfaction had the highest patient satisfaction. Researchers from Kansas State University found that happier people showed better decision-making and job performance.[9] They also had higher levels of physical and emotional wellness which reduced costs to businesses. Principal investigator, Thomas Wright, said, "psychologically well employees are better performers. Since higher employee performance is inextricably tied to an organization's bottom line, employee well-being can play a key role in establishing a competitive advantage." It's been shown that 10–25% of variance in job performance is associated with differences in well-being.[10]

Upside of Investing in Happiness…

Having examined several major drivers of costs related to happiness and well-being, you may wonder about your business' specific ROI in workplace culture. Consider the following observations as a guide to your own analysis.

Deloitte conducted an in-depth review on the ROI for mental health interventions in the workplace, based on twenty-three case

---

[9] Kansas State University "Happy Employees Are Critical For An Organization's Success, Study Shows" in ScienceDaily.
[10] Jennifer Aaker, Sara Gaviser Leslie, and Debra Schifrin "The Business Case for Happiness" – Case No. M345 from the Stanford Graduate School of Business.

studies. They calculated an average return of about a $4 for each $1 spent.[11]

When they analyzed specific interventions, they found that proactive mental health support, such as training and health coaching for managers offered a $6 to $1 return.[12] One well-studied positive psychology training program offers this list of impacts:[13]

a. A 20% increase in engagement scores, the largest increase of any division in a 50,000-employee multinational building materials company.
b. A 50% increase in sales and a decrease in attrition from 12% to 3% over eighteen months (with associated annualized savings of over $1 million).
c. An increase in the percent of people who were happy at work from 43% to 62% and a reduction in the number of people that identified as burned out "often" from 11% to 6%.
d. Healthcare patient experience scores doubled in the following twelve months, transforming a $2 million operating loss into an $8M profit.
e. 10,300 more quotes generated, and 6,500 more sales made than the prior year with the same number of associates in a large insurance brokerage division winning back a client with $12 billion in assets.

Finally, a major research project by Oxford University's Saïd Business School, in collaboration with British multinational telecom

---

[11] Deloitte "Mental health and employers: The case for investment."
[12] Deloitte "Mental health and employers: The case for investment."
[13] The Happiness Advantage: Orange Frog – Success Stories from the International Thought Leader Network.

firm BT, found a conclusive link between happiness and productivity.[14] They asked workers to rate their happiness on a weekly basis for six months using a simple email survey. Attendance, sales conversions, and customer satisfaction were tracked. When all this was analyzed, the researchers found happy workers are 13% more productive.

What would a $6 to $1 return on investment in your people do for your organization? How about a 13% productivity increase across all levels of the organization? What about reductions in absenteeism, turnover, and mental health costs?

The exact impact depends upon your business size, industry, culture, and other factors. But all data points toward a major payoff for investing in happiness and well-being.

Putting a Price on Happiness…

Having discussed the main financial drivers regarding happiness and well-being, you may want to examine a ballpark calculation of how much you could save by investing in culture change. In this example, we'll model a medium-sized insurance company with about three thousand employees. Reasonable estimates show that with a sweeping culture change program that moved the firm from average to exceptional regarding happiness and well-being would cause a bottom-line impact of $29.5 million.

---

[14] Clement Bellet, Jan-Emmanuel De Neve, and George Ward "Does Employee Happiness have an Impact on Productivity?" from Oxford University's Saïd Business School.

Financial Factor	Employees	Savings/Return
Mental Health: Estimate of general mental health costs of $1,560 per employee per year reduced 10% ($156 reduction)	$156 x 3,000 employees =	$468,000
Turnover: 3% reduction in employee turnover with turnover costs of $5,000 per hourly employee and $100,000 per salaried employee. This results in savings of (3% x $5,000) per hourly employee and (3% x $100,000) per salaried employee.	2,000 hourly employees x $150 = $300K 1,000 salaried x $3,000 = $3M	$3,300,000
Absenteeism: Assume reduction in absence of 57%, which is a gain of 3.6 working days per employee. If the average total compensation per employee is $75,000 then divide by 250 working days to get the value of one day's work - $300.	$300 x 3.6 more working days x 3,000 employees =	$3,240,000
Productivity: Assume total compensation is an approximation of an employee's value generation to the business. A 10% increase to average annual compensation of $75,000.	$75,000 x 10% increase x 3,000 employees =	$22,500,000
Total Financial Impact	$29,508,000	

This section isn't an exhaustive analysis or guidebook of how to calculate the ROI of well-being. In fact, we readily admit that exact calculation is rather impractical. But, by now, you should have ample evidence for understanding that happiness and well-being are a mission critical part of business performance.

The bottom line: investing in happiness will improve your bottom line.

Next, let's look at the fundamental ways that workers and their workplaces become happier.

Reflection:

1) Do you know key numbers for your business regarding mental health costs, sick leave, and attrition?
2) In what ways are productivity gains available for your company?
3) What benefits might your organization get in creativity and innovation if your workforce was at its best?

Key takeaways:

1)

2)

3)

Chapter 4

The Unfortunate Truth of Negativity Bias

How often do you enter a social chat with colleagues and quickly discover it's a "venting session"? People are one-upping one another about how bad things are: poor management decisions… inefficient, lazy colleagues… bad market conditions… You've been there, and, if you're anything like me, you've joined in more than a time or two. Why the heck do we do that, and do it a lot?

It doesn't seem to make sense, does it? We don't generally feel good after these sessions, nor do we learn anything new. In fact, it often makes us feel worse, pessimistic, and discouraged.

A negative event, even one of equal weight to a positive event, will have a greater psychological impact.

Negative events stand out. We spend more time contemplating them. There's a physiological greater response from us. We remember them better. They inform more of our decision making.

Negative "stuff" is big. Even our language has an expansive, nuanced choice of words for negative emotions—far more than our vocabulary for positive emotions.[15]

We seem to be hard-wired to pay close attention to negativity. Negativity bias even exists in infants.[16] For example, infants in laboratory experiments show heightened awareness and sensitivity to

---

[15] Robert W. Schrauf, associate professor of applied linguistics at Penn State University in a 2005 interview with Penn State News.
[16] Hamlin, Wynn, and Bloom "3-month-olds show a negativity bias in their social evaluations" published in *Developmental Science* in 2010.

THE UNFORTUNATE TRUTH OF NEGATIVITY BIAS

puppets exposed to danger. This means negativity bias is part of our nature and not simply something we learn.

Being happy is a real challenge when we have an innate, pervasive negativity bias.

No one can say for sure why evolution has wired us to learn more from our negative emotions, but it's true. Most likely, it serves us from a survival perspective. Powerful negative emotions help us navigate the many threats of our pre-agricultural lifestyle:

- **Fear of a predator:** I prepare to fight or run away.
- **Loneliness:** I put more value in the security and support of my social group.
- **Sadness:** I consider the loss I've suffered and take actions to prevent more loss.
- **Anxiety:** I contemplate my future and prepare for eventualities, like winter, food shortages, etc.

Your brain is wired the same as a hunter-gatherer's. Even though struggling to find food or confronting a saber-toothed tiger is exceptionally unlikely today, we remain hyper-attentive to negative stimuli.

Some scholars describe this as "scanning and landing." We continuously search our environments for real and perceived emotional threats. When we spot a "threat," our attention lands on it. And then, in theory, we can problem solve the "threat."

In reality, we typically pay mental and emotional attention to the same emotional hurts repeatedly. We lick our wounds from a broken relationship—sometimes for years, decades even. Or we worry incessantly about some yet unknown future—think financial concerns or health threats… This tendency to dwell on our emotional hurts is mostly a colossal waste of time. It wouldn't be if our survival was truly at risk, but of course, survival in the basic sense of the word is rarely at risk in a modern workplace.

Negativity bias is also an obstacle for workplace happiness. Thankfully, when we understand the role it plays, we can combat it.

Here are three steps you can take:

1) Awareness is the first step: being aware of our bias to view the negative can help us minimize this tendency
2) Do what you can to manage challenges (all manner of bad stuff), then focus on the positive: we don't want to have blind optimism, but a healthy balance between scanning for what's *wrong* and what's *right*
3) Focus on cultivating a positivity bias in your workplace to counteract this natural tendency toward the negative

Research shows we never overcome the negativity bias. Again, this is not about you or people around you being overly pessimistic. Rather it is a shared cognitive bias common to human psychology. *But* despite this fact, we can diminish its impact on our overall disposition if we pay attention to the many positive things we ordinarily take for granted. This is called the Positivity Offset.

With enough *recognized* positive stimuli, we can minimize the negativity bias's overall impact on our emotional state. In business, this means we must design positivity into our day-to-day processes.

We'll discuss this more in Part Three. For now, let's look at how leaders influence the emotional state of their employees.

Reflection:

1) In what ways do you see the negativity bias expressing itself in your life? In your leadership? In your workplace?

2) How do failures, missed targets, mistakes, and other negative events get interpreted by you? By those in our workplace?

Key takeaways:

1)

2)

3)

Chapter 5

Who Dictates Your Culture?
Why Supervisors and Managers Matter

Here is a corporate statement that may seem oddly familiar. "Mission: We build success for all our stakeholders by making our employees our first priority. We are an employer of choice."

Or maybe this one. "Our company is only as good as our people. For that reason, we have only the highest standards of integrity, with excellent pay, benefits and training."

These sound like respectable business pronouncements, right?

The first mission statement comes from a fast-food restaurant that pays most of its workforce a few cents more than minimum wage. And the second statement is one "value" among many from a company that went bankrupt due to repeat health and safety violations that led to major injuries and environmental degradation.

You can imagine the proud C-suite executives and Boards of Directors that endorsed these mission statements. But their operations existed in a reality that was completely out of touch with the publicly heralded statements. I wouldn't be surprised if you've sensed that too: when senior leaders say one thing and the company, in fact, does another.

We might wish our organizations were grounded in genuine, well-crafted vision and mission statements that represent the shared interests and convictions of employees. We want these highly strategic statements of senior leaders to become the signature identity of the business. But mostly, this isn't how it plays out.

WHO DICTATES YOUR CULTURE?

The Greatness Gap—a survey by Achiever's—found that 61% of employees don't know their company's mission statement. And of those that do, 57% aren't motivated by it.[17]

How distant is your culture from the bold mission statement in your business?

Here's the truth. Culture isn't owned by the senior leaders in an organization. Culture is the collective product primarily of frontline employees. It's their beliefs, shared attitudes, and commonly held stories. Culture is the unwritten, and usually unspoken, code of conduct. It's generally taken for granted. For those among it, culture isn't understood; it's unseen and unmanaged. It is what it is: without intention.

Because frontline workers and supervisors create and own culture, most senior leaders struggle to have any impact. They're too distant to even see "it." When they consciously want to shift the culture, they find it difficult. They have few tools with which they can effectively manage culture. Communication initiatives attempt to lead people to a new understanding of the organization. Often this falls flat and cannot sustain itself for long. Worse, staff often cynically reject it as out-of-touch or blatantly manipulative.

Senior leaders can and <u>must</u> lead culture change. This work ought to include a well-timed communication component. But the most overlooked and important leverage for change is your frontline leadership. The immediate supervisors of your workforce hold the key.

Remember, culture is the shared beliefs, attitudes, and collective memories of your staff. These attributes of culture are created and maintained in relationships—simple day-to-day interpersonal connections. The "code of conduct" is how we relate to one another, our customers, and the organization itself. Unless a business is quite

---

[17] Achievers Workforce Institute "The Greatness Gap: The State of Employee Disengagement" 2016 White Paper.

small, there's no way for an executive to connect with employees personally to effect a desired change.

Why are supervisors so strategic? What magic do they possess that they can be the difference makers of culture change?

Consider the quality of their relationships with your frontline.

1. Immediacy—Supervisors are among their subordinates on a near daily basis. They're the practical voice and direction of company leadership.
2. Credibility—The vast majority of supervisors have come from frontline positions themselves. They earned promotions to their current roles because they were good at the work they now oversee. Employees know this and inherently give supervisors respect for their experience and expertise.
3. Intimacy—More than any other level of management, direct supervisors know the operational details, the gripes, and sources of pride for their team members, and, typically, have more than a superficial knowledge about the personal lives of their employees.
4. Relatability—Most supervisors straddle their work identity between being "just another person on the crew" and the "command-and-control leader." They may unhelpfully complain to their personnel about new operational directions. And, at other times, they clearly take charge and enthusiastically bring into reality the vision of their superiors. This ability to be another regular guy or gal on the team *and* a leader makes immediate supervisors relatable, familiar, and trustworthy.

WHO DICTATES YOUR CULTURE?

When it comes to shifting culture, it's this level of supervisory management that provides the <u>only viable source</u> for achieving cultural intentionality. This doesn't mean that senior leaders have no influence. Their active culture management is essential. These senior leaders play a critical role, but it's in their influence over supervisors, not their limited influence over frontline workers, that matters. Therefore, the biggest investment in any culture change must be made in the ranks of supervisors. The focus and determination with which management applies itself to this task is the best indicator of future success or failure.

Reflection:

1) What is your organization's culture? Would your frontline employees agree with your assessment?
2) In your answer above, in what ways is the assessment impacted by the negativity bias?
3) Individually, what role do you play in creating culture? In the context of your position or title, what role do you play in creating culture?

BEYOND PROFIT & PRODUCTIVITY

Key takeaways:

1)

2)

3)

PART TWO

BEYOND MOTIVATION: TOWARD AN ENERGIZED WORKFORCE

Chapter 6

An Office as a Metaphor for Organizational Psychology

Squirrels never ask, "Does my tail make me look fat?" But human beings, with our big, self-examining pre-frontal cortexes, ask egoistic questions all the time. We're concerned with how we are relative to everyone else in the world. How we rank? What makes us unique?

I default to the view that we're fantastically powerful collectively *and* as individuals. But sometimes I need to give myself a reality check. I'm not really "all that and a bag of chips!" How about you? Brace yourself. Here comes a reality check!

Humans – despite all our species' success – are somewhat pathetic as individuals. We're rather puny, unimpressive animals. We don't soar like majestic birds of prey. We haven't got killer qualities like powerful limbs or sharp fangs. We're neither particularly fast, nor do we camouflage into natural settings. As individuals, we're weak, slow, and emotionally needy animals. And it's that last point that makes all the difference.

Those emotions are our weakness and our evolutionary triumph! Emotions give us our survival strength. Emotions bind us with other humans and *only* in tribes (groups of people) do we survive. Meeting our emotional needs as collectives of weak, insignificant individuals led to our success as a species.

Consider our prehistoric ancestors whose brain architecture is the same as ours today. Two hundred thousand years ago, loneliness compelled us to stay close to other members of our tribe. Fear kept us in groups, safe from predators. Emotional rewards, like joy and gratitude, filled us when we successfully hunted or gathered nourishing plants. Love warmed our sense of community long before we figured out how to make and control fire. Meeting our emotional needs was our species' way to ensure we passed on genes from one generation to the next.

We have compelling and constant emotional needs. That's as true today as it was when we were hunter-gatherers. Now, instead of the African savanna, we need our emotional needs met in factories, office towers, retail outlets, and increasingly, remote offices in our homes.

If you recognize and entertain the emotional needs of your workforce, then creating environments where organizations thrive becomes much simpler. A model of human motivations can guide us. Maslow's hierarchy of needs is simple, easy to understand, and has great application to the business world.

Most often, Maslow's hierarchy of needs is depicted as a pyramid. Individuals must meet the lowest level of requirement before they can meet the next highest level. Similarly, the 2nd tier of need must be met before the 3rd. And so on.

I've adapted Maslow's model into a building for workplace psychology and added a sixth level. See the illustration.

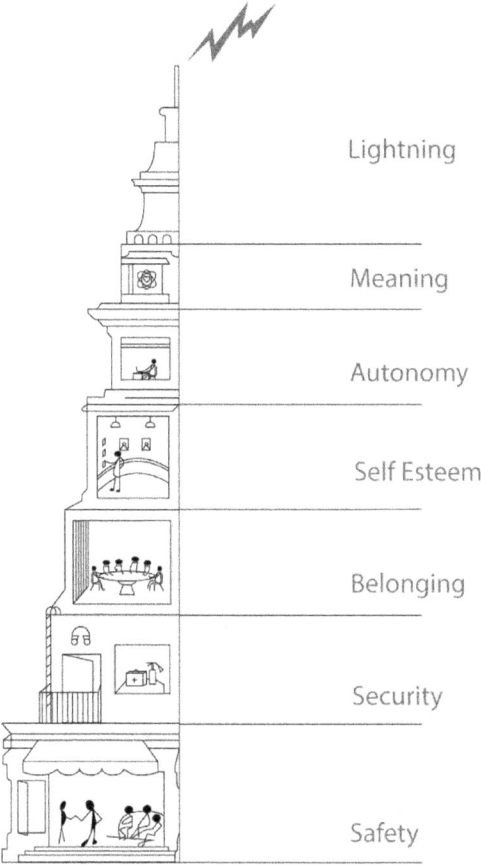

Our workplaces have a fundamental and critical role in meeting the psychological needs of individuals. Let's explore what this looks like.

LOBBY—The harsh lonely elements of wind, rain, and the cold are immediately relieved when you enter through the grand, automated doors of a sophisticated, top-shelf office building. The whoosh of warm, dry air embraces you. A friendly receptionist greets and invites you to help yourself to coffee or tea. You go from bracing against the elements to comfort. This is the level of sustenance.

AN OFFICE AS A METAPHOR FOR ORGANIZATIONAL PSYCHOLOGY

Here we have our *basic needs met*—food, shelter, and clothing. And how do we meet these most basic life requirements in a workplace? You pay your workers so they can afford the necessities of life.

FIRE ESCAPE—The next component of need in a building isn't immediate like food and water, but it's the perceived sense of "I am safe." I may not consider it a lot, but if I realize my building has no way out except the central column of elevator shafts, I'll be uneasy every day I enter the building.

"What if there's a fire? I could die."

"Electricity goes out around here at least once a year. I'll be trapped!"

Yikes! We hate these feelings of a perceived lack of safety, even though the threat (at the moment) isn't real.

This is the level of *security*.

Workers need to know if they get sick, their job will provide for them. They need to believe when they get old, they can stop working. They need to know all the myriad hazards—everything from chemicals in the copier room to five-alarm fires—are managed. We want to know our physical, long-term security is considered and facilitated by our companies.

LUNCHROOM—The next level of need we all share is the need to *belong*. We want to feel like we're a part of a group. And that group has shared interests in common. In the lunchroom, we practice basic human activities such as sharing food, talking about our families, and remarking on the season the local football team is having. We generate genuine connections (beyond work discussions). We grow a sense of community and often become close friends with specific people.

This need for personal connection is about as foundational as it gets. In the absence of a warm, welcoming, metaphorical lunchroom, we're isolated, lonely, and often even paranoid. In the absence of basic human warmth, the workplace is lifeless!

CONFERENCE HALL—Imagine a space outside a large conference room where the photographs of many past and current employees hang in tasteful frames. Sometimes the plaque reads "Top Salesperson," "Team Lead of x, y, z project," or "Chairperson 2010 to 2019." Whatever is said, it's an acknowledgement of the important role that individual is playing, or has played, in the business' life.

If we meet all three previous needs, then there's an opportunity for individuals to have healthy *self-esteem* nurtured in their workplaces. The conference hall is where this happens. Formal acknowledgements happen in the framed photographs, but perhaps even more importantly, frequent informal recognition happens. People exit the conference room, and the VP chats up the last presenter. She talks about what she enjoyed in the presentation, how it's important to her division, and how much she learned. Maybe this brief hallway chatter ends with a big smile and a handshake.

Metaphorical "conference halls" are everywhere in an organization. Wherever work happens, there's an opportunity to meet this incredibly important need for individuals to feel valued. We all want to know our contribution matters, and is noticed, and that our unique talents may shine.

EXECUTIVE OFFICES—Social sciences consistently show interesting findings about people in the most senior positions in an organization. They have very high demands to meet and they self-report high levels of stress. This is identical to typical frontline workers' self-reported perceptions. These folks, just like the executives, feel demands are high, and work is stressful. There's a key difference: executives are far more likely to report a high level of job and life satisfaction relative to the most junior people. Why is there such a big difference?

Executives have a ton of autonomy. They have latitude to pursue projects that interest them. They control their own schedules to a large extent. And they have a feeling that their personal, self-determined convictions matter. They have *autonomy*.

Of course, everyone has limits on their autonomy—even the President of the United States has Congress, the Supreme Court, and voters who keep them in check. Similarly, at every rank in our organizations, there are boundaries to our independent action. But the key emotional learning is this: the degree to which we feel autonomous is causally related to how good we feel about ourselves.

In our workplaces, this means we need to do everything we can to make every worker share in that executive perception of personal autonomy! This is a feeling, not an absolute fact. In the executive offices, we feel we have a choice and a degree of personal self-determination about how we go about our work. The mission is to give all employees this sense of personal autonomy.

ROOFTOP—Oh boy! When we have all our other needs met, we're healthy, happy people. We're flourishing at work. There's only one more thing we really want – that is, to go beyond "making a living" to feel a sense of passion and meaning. We want to escape the toil of "serving the man," step out into the sun, and proudly shout out how we're making the world reflect our own values!

"My work helps keep kids safe!" says the engineer in a car manufacturing company.

"I'm combatting climate change!" beams the salesperson from a solar energy company.

"I'm creating adventure and joy for my customers!" exclaims the travel agent.

It's this feeling of satisfaction you get when the work you do aligns with your personal values that's makes you feel like you're on the rooftop. It doesn't matter what specific values they are. It only matters that individual workers believe their jobs, in some actual way, reflect their own values. You want this. I want this. Everyone wants their work to be meaningful.

LIGHTNING ROD—It's a tall order to have a workforce getting all prior needs met. But when an organization does—BAM! The energy potential is phenomenal! Your workplace will flourish with creativity, productivity, and commitment.

There's still a final level to go. And not all your workers can make it there, but there are special people in every organization that have the potential to be lightning rods.

In geographic locations where lightning storms are frequent, builders include lightning rods on structures. These steel antennas stand above every other aspect of the building. When lightning strikes, it will hit the highest point—the lightning rod—and direct the energy where the builder wants it to go, bypassing the building and safely directing the energy into the ground.

People can do the same thing! Some folks harness energy and radiate it out to those around them magically. This isn't fake, over-the-top positivity or friendliness. In fact, you may not at first recognize them. Positive energizers are as often introverts as they are extroverts. They are individuals in an organization that are critical nodes in the network of spreading positive interpersonal energy. They make a vast difference to businesses and very often have more impact than do people with formal positions of authority and influence.

These lightning rods are available to you. You must find them and unleash their power!

We'll explore these levels of psychological needs for your organization in the following chapters. To be successful as an organization, we need successful, happy workers in an environment where their core psychological needs are met.

Reflection:

1) What levels of needs do you think your organization is meeting?
2) Are your personal needs being met?

Key takeaways:

1)

2)

3)

Chapter 7

THE LOBBY
Meeting Basic Needs

Have you ever been away from home, perhaps on a vacation in a foreign country? Maybe you chose to wander aimlessly. Your feet led you to a residential area with interesting architecture. After a while, unexpectedly, the sun disappears behind a cloud and cool weather blows in. You're cold, shivering, and you didn't bring a sweater. You're miles from your hotel. It's been hours since you last ate. Your feet are tired. Damn! In realizing all this, your interesting morning has gone awry. You hoof it back to the hotel. Emotionally, how do you feel? Tired, a bit vulnerable or desperate, discouraged, and frustrated… Most often that's the emotional condition of those working minimum wage jobs.

Everyone has a primitive drive to come in from the cold, eat a good meal, and sleep in a comfortable bed. We're genuinely impoverished without these. We need to have a lobby to enter. There's an enormous sense of relief and comfort with a familiar place of refuge.

There are a reason people don't generally work for free. We need money to buy things. Without money, we're hungry, naked, and homeless.

The first, most basic need of your workforce is decent pay. Sadly, this isn't as commonplace as we might think.

Since the early 1970s, inflation-adjusted wage rates have frozen. Millennials are the first generation since the Industrial Revolution began who don't expect to be better off economically than their parents.[18] These millennials, along with the newest employees in the workforce (Gen Z), see downward mobility as a genuine possibility. These workers aren't hungry, naked, or homeless, but many in service jobs, retail, and industrial settings are unhappy at work. They're likely working obscene hours to make enough money to make ends meet. They'll leave their employers for the smallest of incremental gains.

With more highly skilled workers, their appetite goes beyond decent compensation. They're looking at amenities offered by more progressive firms. They see workplace gyms, on-site day cares, massages, and meditation rooms as worth moving for.

We think of this first level of Maslow's hierarchy as purely physical. However, it's not that simple. Sociologists have long written about "demonstration poverty." This is the idea that we're constantly comparing ourselves to others who have "more." We feel like we have scarce resources only after seeing others with relatively more resources. Even though I might earn a living wage, with reasonable benefits, I may feel inadequately compensated if I believe the workers next door or in the neighboring city are better off than I am.

Today, with websites like Glassdoor and Indeed, your remuneration and workplace amenities are well known. It's easy to compare your pay package with that of others. To be a desirable employer, you'll need to meet or beat your competitors.

Millennials often endure workplace derision. They're unfairly seen as lazy and disloyal. Consider this generation's reasonable perspective. Corporate America isn't about generous pay and excellent working conditions. The COVID pandemic drove this point home. Legions of low-paid workers in poor conditions became "essential workers," and took on the additional burden of being constantly exposed to a viral pathogen. Think of meat plant workers. They're

---

[18] Cramer, Addo, Campbell, et al. "The Emerging Millennial Wealth Gap" a research primer published by NewAmerica.org.

paid poorly. Their working conditions are wretched. And through the first year of the pandemic, they died disproportionately.

Why should millennials be hard-working and loyal? Their forebears, especially Boomers, entered employment contracts with a completely different set of expectations: jobs for life and an almost certain expectation that their standard of living would be better than their parents'.

Most of the workforce is now made up of millennials. We must pay attention to their valid misgivings about work life. Millennials will give their best, but only if they feel their employer is competitively meeting basic needs. (We'll talk more about this generation in later chapters.)

Lobby: Basic needs met through compensation.

Besides the basic dollars and cents pay, we must not overlook the effect of the physical environment of our businesses. I've been inside literally several hundred office and industrial settings throughout the course of my consulting career. I'm often astonished by the conditions of otherwise successful businesses. Too often, leaders are oblivious to the degree to which their workplaces are pleasing. Are the office chairs rickety and worn? Is the lunchroom clean, comfortable, and functional? I've seen industrial settings with change rooms that stink and have rusting out sinks and mirrors. These physical attributes of workplaces aren't often considered. Plenty of research shows overlooking these aspects of the organizational settings comes at a significant cost to productivity, creativity, and loyalty.

Not only do you need good pay, a clean workplace with quality functional equipment, but you'll also want some comforts and conveniences. In our society where work-life balance is so challenging to achieve, smart employers are getting a leg up on their competition by taking care of their employees.

Think of all the parents who are forced to use substandard daycare that requires an extra ten to twenty minutes of driving on their morning commute. Will they choose to work for an employer with onsite daycare? Yes.

Legions of people pay money to be gym members. How many people would love to have a free onsite, quality gym at their workplace? Millions.

Then there's the iconic image of harried businesspeople at midday dashing out to get a low quality, cheap bite of food from a street vendor so they can rush back to their high-pressure jobs. How grateful are workers who have free, or highly subsidized, healthy food options right in their own building? Beyond pleased.

Employers ought to make environments of convenience, fun, health, fitness, and social connection. There are plenty of creative ways to achieve this. Here are a few ideas:

- Daycares
- Gyms
- Cafeterias and free snacks well distributed
- Arcades with video and physical games
- Meditation rooms
- Nap rooms
- Expansive outdoor decks with plenty of social spaces

With a little thought and genuine desire, organizations can invest in competitive pay, supportive workspaces where form and function further productivity, and an array of amenities that feel like daily bonuses. With good attention given to meeting the basic needs of workers, your organization can move on to meeting the psychological security needs of your workforce, which is the next chapter's subject.

Reflections:

1) How does your organization compare regarding pay and benefits?
2) What's your workplace doing well regarding amenities beyond compensation?

Actions:

1)

2)

3)

Chapter 8

The Fire Escape
Meeting Perceived Must-haves

You never want to use the fire escape, but when you think about it, you sure are glad there is one!

In the prior chapter, we discussed the immediate, tangible needs for our basic wellbeing. Our physiological requirements, which money allows us to meet, are essential. In the absence of a promise of pay, workers won't show up. The second level in our hierarchy of needs is nearly as essential. Like getting caught out in the cold on a morning walk, when our basic needs aren't met, we feel it – the same applies to security needs.

Your staff has a need for perceived security in terms of their organization's safety program, health insurance, freedom from layoffs, and retirement plans.

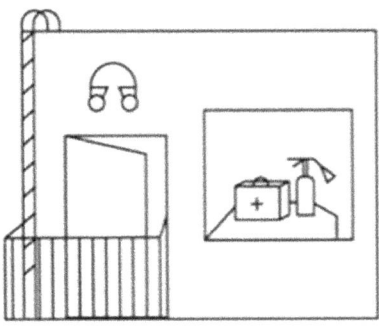

Fire Escape: Feeling of security (physical, financial, job)

Physical Security

We need to believe we're safe. If we're not feeling safe, we'll anxiously attempt to secure our environment, or we will leave to find someplace else where we feel safer.

Early in my career, my focus was accident prevention in other employers' workplaces. With few exceptions, when workers felt their employers did a poor job of ensuring a safe workplace, morale was terrible—it was beyond low. There was often an open rebellion. Many workers actively sought to harm their employer—unconsciously pursuing vigilante justice.

Often, the perception of safety differed vastly from one workplace to the next. One company's culture accepted that a lot of physical risks are inherent in their industry; whereas another employer in the same line of work might have an objectively better safety program, but their staff perceived a neglect of safety.

Very often, I encountered employers who were committed to excellence in health and safety but didn't have an adequate practical implementation of safety programming. The firms that were committed, yet did a poor job of implementation, were held in contempt by the workforce just as much as the firms that simply didn't care about safety.

This disparity between cultures clarifies that the distinction is in the workers' perceptions. Obviously, I advocate for real, implemented programs of safety. But, from a purely cultural perspective, it's the workforce's beliefs that matter.

As a consultant, I once helped a desperate, family-run business with a profound safety problem. The organization suffered five fatalities from five separate incidents in one calendar year. This company did work in a very hazardous industry—forestry. And they did this work in the toughest of conditions: old-growth forests in the steep mountains of British Columbia. Nevertheless, five tragic deaths devastated the company and the entire community in which it operated. There was no excuse. Each death was preventable.

The five fatalities occurred even though their safety program, as written, resulted in a "maximum achievement reward" of a 5% discount on their workers' compensation insurance premiums. What a shocking contradiction!

To rectify this, we trained frontline supervisors in several soft skills you'll read about later in this book. We also measured how frequently leaders talked about safety as a normal, everyday part of productivity and quality conversations. The process was methodical and consistent. It took effort and focus; however, this wasn't rocket science!

With a purely cultural intervention, the company enjoyed a 92% reduction in unsafe behaviors. None of our interventions had anything to do with their formal safety program. The interventions were entirely interpersonal. I'm proud to say that to the present day, the company is now a safety leader.

Health Security

Workers must feel their life and limbs are being taken care of before they can consistently commit creative, abundant effort to their jobs. This importance of perceived physical safety also speaks to the need for health insurance. In countries without a robust national healthcare system (most notably absent in the USA), workers will be hesitant to maintain an employment relationship with an organization that isn't meeting this desire for security.

Job Security

The need for job security is just like the desire for safety from physical risks. It's tolerable when absent, but only to a degree. It's all well and fine to know I'm earning a paycheck this week, maybe this month, but if I have uncertainty about the next month, or six months from now, I may have constant subconscious anxiety. This is especially true in the middle portion of our careers—roughly twenty-eight- to fifty-five-years-old. Through this period, we're raising children, paying mortgages, and trying to "make it" in society. Chronic insecurity about employment is especially detrimental to our well-being in those years.

Financial Security

It's also through the same period, we ought to consider our long-term financial security. If we're not managing our savings, profound anxiety grows with each passing year as we progress toward retirement age (whatever that may be). Sadly, many people mismanage their money even when pay is sufficient for savings. For this reason, organizations that contribute to 401(k)s or otherwise have pensions as part of their benefit package, significantly increase their workforce retention.

People will stay with an employer to meet several security needs. The first two levels within our hierarchy of needs are basic in many respects. They're easy to understand, and they're grounded in very tangible realties—life and limb physicality. The levels we turn to are emotional, intangible, often overlooked, and therefore usually left to happenstance.

Reflections:

1) What is your personal assessment of your security needs? How does your work succeed or fail in supporting these needs?
2) How is your organization doing in meeting these basic security needs? Noting that these needs are psychological, are there simple ways your organization could increase the *feeling* of or perception of security in your workforce?

Actions:

1)

2)

3)

Chapter 9

Lunchroom
Belonging and Connecting with Groups

Do you remember your high school cafeteria? Doing so will either bring back good memories or poor ones. The lunchroom was a place of intense social dynamics. Cliques of all kinds existed. You probably sat with the same kids at the same table day after day. New kids, or socially isolated kids, would wander in with their tray, scanning the large room for some place to sit. It was awkward and brought all kinds of vulnerability and insecurity to the surface.

The lunchroom is a metaphor for the place where we find our social connection at work. There are, of course, many places that facilitate people becoming friends with one another. We all need friends. We need our workplaces to create opportunities for social connection.

Often, we (mistakenly) believe that humans' big brains evolved so we could be smart—technically advanced relative to other species. We have this huge part of our brain—the prefrontal cortex—that makes us quite unlike most every other species. And that huge chunk of gray matter gives us language, agriculture, and even rockets that fly into outer space. Naturally, this must be the reason our brains developed the way they did over many thousands of years.

Wrong!

There's plenty of evidence that 200,000 years ago the utility of our big brains was for the sophisticated management of complex tribal relationships.[19] Technology was absent, but the need to *belong*

---

[19] Robin Dunbar "The social brain hypothesis and its implications for social evolution" published in *Annals of Human Biology* 2009.

was everywhere. Our brains evolved the way they did for us to be successful socially. Almost all this happens, then and now, at a subconscious level.

We read each other's emotions through myriad ways, including *mirror neurons*. These are brain cells that see emotions on other's faces then express those same emotions on our face. These mirror neurons work fast. In as little as 33 milliseconds (33 one-thousandths of a second) we see emotion and reflect it back.[20] This happens pre-cognitively; that means before we're consciously aware of taking someone else's emotions, they become our own. Scientists refer to this stunning phenomenon as *emotional contagion*.

Can you see the use of this? If someone in our tribe sees a threat, such as a tiger approaching, that person shows fear and alarm. Long before they say anything, other members of the tribe subconsciously observe this fear and alarm and take on these same emotions instantly. We run or we fight *together*. Collectively, we share emotions so we can survive.

Why is loneliness one of the most painful emotions? Because it powerfully instructs us to cleave and commit to our tribe. Why is laughter contagious? Because it enhances social cohesion and creates bonds of camaraderie. We're complicated emotional beings, so that we can function superbly in groups.

Our tribal nature isn't a function of social conditioning or life circumstance. It's hard-wired into us. *From a well-being perspective, it's as important to our mental health as food is for our physical health.* An organization must recognize this need and consciously foster a culture of belonging. We must facilitate human bonding, collaboration, and teamwork.

---

[20] Hyeonjin Jeon and Seung-Hwan Lee "From Neurons to Social Beings: Short Review of the Mirror Neuron System Research and Its Socio-Psychological and Psychiatric Implications" in *Clinical Psychopharmacology and Neuroscience* 2018.

Frontline managers (immediate supervisors) are critical to creating belonging. This is a deeply personal construct. It can't be brought about by declarations from the Human Resources department. Policies against bullying, sexism, and racism — while important — don't connect people. Statements about workplace respect don't generate warm bonds of trust. These kinds of HR initiatives are helpful, but individual leaders must have the skills to engage with their staff genuinely. Their emotional intelligence matters.

Organizations must be attentive to the many direct reports assigned to leaders, as meaningful relationships are difficult to develop when supervisors are spread too thin. Supervisors must thoroughly understand that they're leaders of people and not merely production managers. Leaders must show a genuine interest in their team members. Warm greetings and curiosity about someone's personal life go a long way.

I remember in my corporate career when I was still together with my ex-wife. In the summer of 2008, my wife's mom was dying of cancer. Her mother was in her end days. My wife, Rosemary, decided she needed to support her family as her mother was dying. It was the right thing to do.

I immediately booked off all three weeks of my remaining allotted vacation. Rosemary moved back into her parents' house, which was a two-hour drive away. And I took full-time care of our two sons (seven and ten years-old). A problem arose when I ran out of vacation, and, most unexpectedly, Rosemary's mom hadn't passed. Rosemary and her family were still holding vigil over her mother's bed. What could I do?

Obviously, Rosemary couldn't return to provide full-time care for our kids.

I told my boss what was going on. "Alex, I'm out of vacation time, but I can't come back just yet. My family needs me."

Without hesitation, he told me to see the process through. "Paul, take the time you need. Focus on what's important." And, with sincere warmth, he added: "Family is everything."

The organization paid for the additional week before life gave way to death. It was a professional experience of compassion and grace I've always cherished. I got the support my family needed from my employer when it was needed most.

This may seem obvious, but great leaders send flowers when people are sick and welcome them when they return to work. They celebrate their employees' personal milestones in a friendly, sincere way. They show solidarity and empathy when people meet life's inevitable tragedies. If connecting with subordinates feels unnatural to some of your leaders, they may be a poor fit for their role.

With conscientious intention, businesses can facilitate connection.

Put common spaces, like a lunchroom or gym, in areas of natural light. Good lunchroom amenities draw people into them. Kitchen tools, appliances, and open countertops are attractive in their utility. Seating should be cozy and comfortable. Designers can deliberately create small group spaces within the seating areas. Some variety is useful—dining tables, couches, TV's (with the sound off), and high-top tables with seating for two or three. Common spaces are more attractive with plants, art, and soothing sound (or at least relatively quiet).

In industrial settings, the design elements of natural, friendly environments are even more important. Soundproofed meeting rooms can be next to loud factory floors. Locker rooms should be spa like, setting a space that's relaxing, pleasing, and more than simply utilitarian.

This kind of design isn't expensive, it just requires thoughtfulness.

If emotionally intelligent, engaging supervisory staff is priority one, and supportive physical spaces priority two, the third area of attention is formal social planning. Organizations can encourage belonging in several creative ways. We can arrange lunchtime classes on various subjects; ideally with some lessons taught by volunteer staff members. Think exercise classes, art, languages, cooking, meditation, and technology. (Not a boring lunch and learn...) Consider your workforce. Is English as a second language important? Do your workers want to navigate the process to achieve citizenship, and would they enjoy practical help achieving it? Does your company's savings program require personal knowledge of investment strategies? Design programs relevant to your people — make them fun and interesting.

Does your organization do work in the community? This is an effective social bonding opportunity. Could your workforce build a playground if the business bought the equipment? Are there environmental projects, such as beach cleanups, that would inspire volunteerism? What would rally your people? Perhaps there's a large charity your organization could get behind. The more we delegate this kind of social planning to enthusiastic staff who cheerfully get on board, the better. However, some ongoing employer facilitation and management is required.

Belonging: quality relationships, being connected

LUNCHROOM BELONGING AND CONNECTING WITH GROUPS

When your employees feel that they're part of a genuinely connected group, they identify with their "people." They have workmates they consider friends (even if they're only seen at work). Belonging to a workplace massively increases commitment and motivation. People volunteer their best efforts to give to their "tribe," — their organization. You have the opportunity to facilitate a sense of belonging which will drive unified engagement from the people in your organization.

We turn next to the wish among all people who want to feel good about themselves—to have genuine self-esteem.

Reflections:

1) What genuine friendships have you cultivated at work? How did they form?
2) What's your assessment of your workplace's awareness of the need for belonging?
    a. Does it hire people-oriented leaders?
    b. To what degree is the physical environment supportive of positive socializing?
    c. What programming is specifically designed to bond the members of your workforce?

Actions:

1)

2)

3)

Chapter 10

Conference Hall
Self-esteem and Knowing One's Own Value

A colleague told me a story about starting her corporate career as a bank teller and being promoted to the role of customer service representative.

One day, her district manager arrived for a meeting and told my friend and all her colleagues they were expendable and easily replaceable. In one sentence, the district manager completed destroyed any desire my colleague had to go the extra mile for the company. From then on, she did the bare minimum. Her personal contribution was the opposite of enthusiastic. It shocked me when I heard her story, as she's one of the hardest working people I know. She always goes above and beyond to serve her clients. And, like so many people, this committed, high-energy woman is naturally that way.

What harm do we inflict in our workplaces when we diminish, ridicule, and ignore our employees? It is so obviously counterproductive.

It feels good to see ourselves as worthy of honor and recognition. On some level, we all want our picture nicely framed and hung in the conference hall.

After our need for physical safety, a sense of security, and belonging to one or more social groups is met, we all have certain self-esteem requirements. When we inquire about our value, we need an affirming answer. We need to feel our contribution matters, that our presence makes a meaningful difference.

Tragically, many workplaces do little to meet this need. Layers of pointless bureaucracy defeat any sense of personal contribution. Individuals become nameless, faceless cogs in an inefficient, dull machine. Similarly, some workplaces have leadership cultures that devalue the people who do the productive work of the business—they see frontline staff as interchangeable and individually unimportant. This causes workers to become cynical—the employer becomes unimportant… a means to an end and unworthy of loyalty and respect.

Healthy self-esteem is something we naturally pursue. When we have it, we feel good about ourselves. It's energizing. Our positive beliefs in our capacity to contribute empower us. We make greater contributions because we believe we can. A workforce made up of people with good feelings about themselves is powerful.

Just as there are organizations that habitually diminish self-esteem, there are others that enhance it. It's often difficult to know how well we're doing in our personal lives. Rating our performance as a parent, lover, friend, neighbor, etc., can be difficult, especially for someone with low self-esteem. What clear goal posts are there? How do we define success in our social relationships? Is there a scoreboard? For many people, the one place they feel best about themselves is at work.

Work can be exceptionally good at reinforcing positive feelings. Where structure and routine may be lacking in one's personal life, work often has clear expectations: starting times, scheduled breaks, lunch, and the end of each shift. Well managed workplaces keep score: productivity is measured objectively, quality is defined, and our work often has an easily understood outcome—product A, or service B. These attributes of work are excellent if the criteria are fair and achievable. We all want to know how we're doing. When the definition of "good work" is especially clear, we facilitate abundant self-esteem. This ability to assess for one's own self is important.

Conference Hall: Self-esteem through respect & recognition

There are two kinds of self-esteem—one that relies on the input of others and one that's self-determined. The former is okay. The latter is more robust.

If my ego needs depend on others' views, I may often feel inadequate. I need notoriety—maybe even fame. Praise and validation are what I crave the most. I want others to recognize my status. I want to rank higher than my coworkers. I want awards, special assignments, and privileges. If I don't confidently value my worth, I seek my self-esteem from others. I'll probably never have "enough."

If someone has a healthy self-regard, it's inherently self-determined. She is confident. She knows she has a mastery over her core responsibilities. She knows she's succeeding internally. To foster this internal self-esteem, we must provide clear expectations and measures of success. Workplaces, more so than fluid non-work settings, can and should help people gauge their performance accurately.

Can you define "productive" work for each position at your firm? What does "quality" entail? And to what end is each person working? Without knowing these attributes, workers will flounder and will be more likely to have poor self-esteem.

Creating clear criteria for success may be more obvious for some kinds of work than for others. Someone assembling physical items, or fulfilling warehouse orders, may perfectly understand success and failure. Professionals, such as accountants, managers, and lawyers, may have a harder time seeing their measures of success. If their superiors can't help them get clear about these roles, their outcomes, and their measures of productivity and quality, then the organization is failing these valuable members of their workforce.

Every worker deserves to know what success looks like and they deserve to know it in a form that doesn't rely on others' opinions. We want to assess our own outcomes confidently.

Once roles and measures of performance are clear, there are other ways organizations can bolster self-esteem.

Appreciation and Recognition

"Thank you." "Good job." "Well done." "Way to go!" "Fantastic work!" "Exceptional performance!" "Gosh, I appreciate the difference you make!"

We all like to hear these statements from coworkers, especially our supervisors. Yet, it's rather remarkable that in one Gallup survey, 65% of employees said they hadn't received recognition at all that year.[21] A different study from Southern Methodist University said workers need to be recognized for good work within the week they did it.[22] It seems we have a lot of room for improvement.

Frequent, sincere words of appreciation go a long way toward improving workplace morale.

---

[21] Donald O. Clifton, Ph.D. "Be Nice: It's Good for Business" a 2004 Q&A with Tom Rath

[22] Lorea Seidel "Good Job! How to Give Recognition That Promotes Outstanding Performance" SMU Human Resources Blog 2010

Public Celebrations

Some employees don't want to be publicly recognized, and it's valuable to be sensitive to that. However, overall, it's great to make a big deal about good performance.

When an individuals' and/or a team's performance is meeting all your targets, it's time to say, "HOORAY!" We ought to understand that pay is the mechanism for meeting physical needs. But money is NOT as motivating for outstanding performance as sincere recognition. Calling attention to great work instills a level of pride that dollars and cents never will.[23] A cake and a few choice words can be a definite career highlight, whereas most pay raises are quickly forgotten. I don't want to be dismissive of compensation; a good chunk of bonus money AND a public celebration may be the *best* combination.

Real Recognition—Witnessing

While "thanks" and a pat on the back *are* valuable, there's a way of doing it that's more effective than merely saying "thanks for your good work." In a society with oversized cynicism, we dismiss praise as superficial. "Thanks" outside of any real context can be easily devalued.

You can tell someone how awesome they are without a single word of thanks and be a hundred times more powerful in boosting their self-esteem. This is simple. We all want to be seen, heard, and understood. You do this by describing in some detail what you observed that's so praiseworthy.

---

[23] There is nothing wrong with performance bonuses per se, but many studies show that financial incentives are not fabulous motivators for great work.

CONFERENCE HALL SELF-ESTEEM AND KNOWING ONE'S OWN VALUE

Look at the difference in these two types of feedback following the same successful sale:

1) Great job on getting the new account! I really appreciate the hard work. You hit it out of the park on this one. Thanks so much.
2) Wow. I see you landed the new account. The sheer tenacity it took is remarkable. You put in weeks of work to win this valuable new client. I know there were many objections to overcome. You patiently answered all their questions. You convinced them of our superior quality by letting them demo our product. Getting their signature on the contract and having our production team already filling their order is huge. Long term, this contract is worth a fortune to our division. Your hard work is making a substantial difference. You must feel very proud.

By detailing how the salesperson won the new contract and stating why the sale is important, you're reflecting on their success to them. In the first scenario, you provide your opinion of their performance. They'll get a lift in spirit through your praise. In the second scenario, you recognized their work. Through your words, they can see for themselves how valuable they are. Their internal sense of self-esteem grows.

People want to be deeply witnessed. Consider the bizarre way many people lay their lives on social media. They crave positive recognition for who they are. But "likes" and "views" are superficial. By contrast, specific feedback contributes to powerful self-esteem enhancement. It motivates. It builds loyalty. And it's seen as sincere, personal, and meaningful.

It's beyond the scope of this book, but as an expert in positive psychology, and an executive coach, a lot of my one-on-one work is done in this space of deep witnessing. With at least half of my coaching clients, when they reach out, there's a distinct lack of confidence underlying some aspect of their work and/or life mission. These individuals are extraordinarily talented, capable leaders. But no one is powerfully witnessing their strengths and describing the processes that led to so much success. Good coaches hold up accurate mirrors, so their clients see themselves at their best. We can all learn to do this for our workmates. We get better at it with practice!

In our building metaphor, we now have safe, secure, socially connected, and proud employees! In the next chapter, we'll discuss how to make them self-starters on a personal mission to make big contributions to the organization.

Reflections:

1) What does your organization do to enhance self-esteem in its employees? What do you do?
2) What does your organization do that diminishes self-esteem? Think deeply on this one; cultural deficits aren't always readily visible. What do you do?
3) What avenues of enhancing self-esteem are most valuable to you personally?

Actions:

1)

2)

3)

Chapter 11

Executive Offices
Self-Actualization One of Two: Autonomy

When all our other needs are met, we want to transcend work and express ourselves through our professional lives. We want to feel the sun and open our arms wide as we breathe deeply feeling as though we're on top of the world.

Self-actualization is the highest need in Maslow's hierarchy. We must satisfy all four prior needs before an individual can deeply express themselves. When we use our skills and talents in a way that feels intrinsically motivating, we are self-actualized. Our work becomes an expression of who we are. It's our contribution to the world. We can only do this if we feel a sense of autonomy.

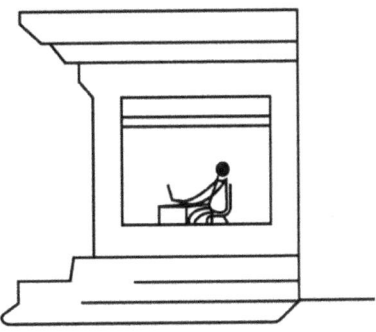

Executive Offices: Autonomy and expression of one's potential.

This desire for self-direction and self-expression may be the most difficult need for a workplace to meet. Self-actualization isn't about the deliverables of a business. Instead, it's an individual's stand for themselves—it's a creative expression of an intrinsic urge. When the intrinsic urge aligns with the organization's interests, magic happens!

Imagine a marketing agency looking for creative, out of the box ideas that can break through the cluttered landscape of advertising. A copywriter allowed his own process may come up with brilliant ideas. He may be unorthodox, perhaps even difficult to manage. But the quality of his work is truly exceptional — winning big accounts repeatedly. Would a lucky employer make accommodations for this individual? Will his unorthodox process be not only tolerated, but encouraged? Would odd working hours be acceptable? Could he dribble a basketball and shoot hoops in his office? Would his colleagues willingly sit through some occasional meetings and theatrics to facilitate his thinking style? These are reasonable accommodations in this business setting, but how well do similar scenarios play out in other settings?

An organization should give as much autonomy as it can to each employee. How that looks will vary from one workplace to the next, and from one employee to the next.

When a worker has a job with many rote requirements, autonomy seems elusive. Consider a factory worker repetitively assembling a precise mechanical component part for an automobile. Creative self-expression is mostly unavailable regarding the assembly process. Still, there are a lot of ways an organization can facilitate self-actualization.

Consider how the requirements can be minimized and how options may be expanded. Perhaps the order in which assembly is done may be mandatory. The tightness of fasteners — mandatory. Safety precautions — mandatory. Zero compromise is likely necessary in these areas. But where are their possibilities for intrinsic motivations?

Would earbuds with a personal selection of music be okay? Are there options for work gloves to pick from? Could the worker organize their tools and workspace as they see fit? All these small areas of potential choice shouldn't be taken for granted. Cumulatively, choosing for oneself may significantly improve the culture of the workplace.

How we engage with this worker is especially important. If they've accumulated expertise, how can the employer respect them as a knowledgeable person? Are they part of the process review? Do they help develop quality measures? Are they consulted about safety programs? When the worker is a part of the conversation, and their input is truly valued, their self-actualization is supported.

On the other end of the work process continuum, consider highly experienced white-collar professionals. The best practices of their profession should dictate their constraints. For example, your accountants follow the prescribed practices identified by their professional governing body. Beyond that, their work should be measured nearly exclusively by outcomes.

A common mistake is to prescribe processes for professional staff. Companies do this because some employees do low quality work. Therefore, organizations respond by making all members of a job classification take on an ever-growing list of "must-dos."

- Check this box when a customer called.
- Complete this memo for noting cost benefit analysis.
- Use 12-point Times New Roman font on Form x237.
- On Fridays, do expense sheets.
- "Don't forget the cover page for the TPS reports. ☺"

And on and on and on.

Layers of bureaucratic requirements pile up. For many large organizations, institutional memory often isn't available to explain why the process is what it is. As a result, it's shamefully inefficient and deals progressively more blows to worker morale.

Contrast this with more agile businesses. There are few processes, except those that assist in consistency and quality. We all understand the need for bureaucracy. It keeps chaos at bay. However, there are bureaucracies that promote positive work cultures, and they don't emphasize work processes. Instead, they measure results.

Teach best practices for customer service. For example, with few, if any, required processes. Zappos, a famously positive workplace, has no scripts for call center sale staff. Instead, employees are instructed to serve customers as best they can. Zappos is primarily in the business of shoes sales. The late founder of the company, Tony Hsieh, famously tells this story in his book *Delivering Happiness*:

> *I'm reminded of a time when I was in Santa Monica, California, a few years ago at a Skechers sales conference. After a long night of bar-hopping, a small group of us headed up to someone's hotel room to order some food. My friend from Skechers tried to order a pepperoni pizza from the room-service menu but was disappointed to learn that the hotel we were staying at did not deliver hot food after 11:00pm. We had missed the deadline by several hours.*
>
> *In our inebriated state, a few of us cajoled her into calling Zappos to try to order a pizza. She took us up on our dare, turned on the speakerphone, and explained to the (very) patient Zappos rep that she was staying in a Santa Monica hotel and really craving a pepperoni pizza, that room service was no longer delivering hot food, and that she wanted to know if there was anything Zappos could do to help.*
>
> *The Zappos rep was initially a bit confused by the request, but she quickly recovered and put us on hold. She returned two minutes later, listing the five*

closest places in the Santa Monica area that were still open and delivering pizzas at that time.

Now, truth be told, I was a little hesitant to include this story because I don't want everyone who reads this book to start calling Zappos and ordering pizza. But I just think it's a fun story to illustrate the power of not having scripts in your call center and empowering your employees to do what's right for your brand, no matter how unusual or bizarre the situation.

As for my friend from Skechers? After that phone call, she's now a customer for life.

Be like Zappos! Measure customer service outcomes continuously and let the process take care of itself.

Objective measures of performance are motivating, and don't reduce autonomy. Be explicitly clear about your quality standards and how they're determined, then prescribe minimal steps to achieve them. Set productivity expectations and sit back and observe the outcomes. Professionals may often want to negotiate performance expectations. This is great. They know their workload, competing demands, and the nature and complexity of their projects best. If, following discussion, there's consensus on expected outcomes, there's tremendous likelihood individuals will be eager to meet or exceed targets.

Have you ever worked for an insecure manager who was all too enthusiastic to monitor you and your workmate's every move? Your micro-manager supervisor was over-bearing, annoying, and stood in the way of getting stuff done. They probably robbed any creativity from your team and drained motivation like a sieve.

When interacting with experienced professionals, take the role of student. Have your staff teach you about their field of expertise, why they're approaching their assignments the way they are, and what outcomes they hope to achieve. Ask good questions! If you're satisfied, as their supervisor, with what you've been taught, ask, "how can I help?" In this way, you're enhancing self-actualization. Make space for your people's wisdom, talents, and expertise. THEN measure outcomes continuously.

What more could there be? Employees getting all their needs met must be ecstatic. But wait, there's one more requirement before you've met all the psychological requirements for a flourishing workplace. In the next chapter, we'll examine meaning and purpose.

Reflections:

1) What's the balance of your workplace between necessary bureaucracy and empowering autonomy?
2) Consider your role; does it support your self-direction and self-expression? How do you support this in the people you manage directly?

Actions:

   1)

   2)

   3)

Chapter 12

Rooftop
Self-Actualization Two of Two—Meaning

Have you ever been in burnout mode—even briefly? Your work, through cumulative burden, has become depersonalized. You go through the motions, but you left your heart at home a long time ago. You don't feel like your efforts make any difference. You feel like nothing important will change. And, most tragically, you feel your own contribution is meaningless — devoid of any soul. This depressing state is incredibly common. In fact, about half the working population in the U.S. show many signs of burnout.[24]

A happy workforce must feel like their jobs are purposeful and connected to their own values.

Meaning didn't use to be important in the workplace. Boomers, and the following generation—Gen X (born 1965–1980)—grew up with an expectation that they'd have long-term employment with one or two large, stable companies. As a loyal, reasonably talented individual, a person could expect to achieve several promotions and pay raises. Over a career, the economic quality of life would gradually improve until you gracefully retired with an adequate nest egg tucked away.

As mentioned in Chapter Seven, generational differences are changing the workplace.

Millennials, born between 1980 and 2000, are the dominant force in workplace culture. This demographic makes up one half of the workforce. They grew up with an entirely different set of adult

---

[24] Jack Kelly "Indeed Study Shows That Worker Burnout Is At Frighteningly High Levels: Here Is What You Need To Do Now" in Forbes 2021.

career expectations. They observed that real wage growth flatlined. Average earnings are the same today as they were in 1974 (adjusted for inflation). For the first time since the Industrial Revolution began, one generation (millennials) can't expect a higher standard of living than their parents. Indeed, a recent study[25] shows that for children born in 1980, when they turned thirty, less than 50% of them were better off than their parents were on their thirtieth birthdays. Downward mobility is a real and not unreasonable expectation for millennials and the generation now in college — Gen Z.

Poor economic prospects aren't the only perspective-shifting reality impacting younger generations. Millennials grew up seeing their parents live through the "dot-com" bubble of 2002. Remember that? Technology companies grew fast. Their innovations and computer-based tools seemed to be the answer for everything. Mergers and acquisitions were rampant. The 1990s saw massively escalating stock prices for tech, attracting ridiculous market valuations that proved unsustainable. A huge market correction and the resulting fallout saw hundreds of thousands of layoffs of well-educated, upwardly mobile professionals. We went from believing in a world where our single employer would keep us for life, to a dog-eat-dog world where a career might include a dozen or more employers, mixed with periods of time immersed in the gig economy. The gig economy is, too often, a pseudo-entrepreneurial environment notable for instability and lots of low-wage competition.

Given these coming-of-age conditions for millennials and Gen Z, is it any wonder that they're seen as less loyal workers? Who can blame them? Unlike prior generations, they're not promised loyalty from their employers. And they can't count on the same standard of living their parents did. Older generations, with the promise of stable,

---

[25] Ray Chetty, et. al, The Fading American Dream: Trends in Absolute Income Mobility Since 1940, National Bureau of Economic Research working paper 22910, December 2016.

progressively higher paying jobs, made an unwritten commitment to their employer: "give me steady work with opportunity for advancement and I'll do what you want." Boomers and X-Gens didn't demand fulfilling and personally meaningful work. They didn't expect their companies to be good for the environment, to make valuable contributions to society, or otherwise advance the greater good. In general, Boomers and X-Gens didn't feel that their employers had to address their personal values as a component part of their workplace culture. Now, it's important to point out that plenty of folks in older generations value meaning and purpose. But speaking in generalities, in the past there was not the same expectation for personal fulfillment that there is today.

Millennials and Gen Z expect meaningful work.

They aren't selling their labor for pay; at least not in the simplistic way prior generations did. Millennials know employers are making few promises to them. As a result, they want roles that mean something—jobs that truly align with their values.

Did you know that 33% of millennial employees quit their jobs within the first ninety days?[26] One can reasonably expect that these new hires knew the pay they'd receive and had a fairly clear idea of the tasks they'd be expected to do. So, what causes them to leave? Something feels wrong to them. They don't like command-and-control leaders. The work culture is stifling and boring. New hires often stop learning shortly after being trained for a process-driven job. And they see little opportunity for personal growth. Summing this up: they find the work devaluing and devoid of meaning — soul-sucking.

---

[26] 2018 Jobvite survey of over 1500 millennials.

ROOFTOP SELF-ACTUALIZATION TWO OF TWO—MEANING

Interestingly, although millennials brought this need for meaning to the workplace, it's grown in appeal, so more and more boomers and X-Gens want their jobs to feel soulful.

The pursuit of meaning is an individual's drive to live a life consistent with their highest values. If I grew up with strong environmental values, and my company is destroying the environment, I quit. If I value a sense of adventure and my company culture is staid, boring, and predictable, I quit. If I align myself with social causes like eliminating racial inequality, and my employer has nothing but white people in the C-Suite, I quit. If I'm a strong supporter of community involvement, and my company has zero visible initiatives to give back to the community, I quit. And even if my organization is environmentally responsible, playful in its entrepreneurialism, dedicated to diversity, and active in community projects, if I don't feel it as an employee, then yes, I quit.

Younger generations especially, and all generations, want to feel like their work connects them to their personal values. They want their work to contribute to a personal sense of purpose and meaning. In the absence of purpose and meaning, workers are without self-actualization. If good options are available, they'll jump ship to another employer. If no job opportunities exist, they may stay, contribute as paid to do, and never commit wholeheartedly to their job. Or worse, they'll join the significant proportion of the workforce who Gallup classifies as "actively disengaged." They believe their values are diametrically opposed to their workplace's values. They believe the culture of the organization is contemptible. These are the people sabotaging the success of their organizations.

Rooftop: Meaning through living one's values

Self-actualization is an inside job. As noted previously, it's not an easy task for an employer to meet this need. However, there are practical mechanisms that make the odds much, much better.

Make the End-users of Your Products and Services Visible

In many workplaces, the people who toil to create and support products or services are far removed from the people who benefit from the business' outputs. For example, I led the implementation of a culture change project in a pulp mill.

The stinky, dilapidated industrial site produced raw materials that were shipped all over the world. The small town where the mill is situated was both far in distance and in spirit from end users. The company made a specialty paper that left the mill as a tiny white pellet.

Manufacturers in Asia made a variety of products with these white pellets. Notably, one company made diapers—the pellets were absorptive. Another company produced bandages designed to slow-release prescription medications. After I asked some leading questions, the mill's executive leaders realized the need to connect the workforce with consumers. So, we began a low-cost, effective campaign to bring the end users closer to the mill's employees. Mostly, this comprised education and some simple internal communications. Posters, for example, were made of mothers holding newborn babies in diapers. Another poster had a doctor applying the patch that delivered medication. Suddenly, the mill was much more than a paycheck. It was about family and health. The work being done made a positive difference in the world. Who can't identify with those values?

Community Support

Research shows we give more generously to causes we identify with. Sponsoring a local sports team may go much further than an annual United Way drive (as wholesome as that may be). A workforce will see "their" kids in the local paper. See the discussion in Chapter 8 about organizing a singular, major local charity initiative. A client of mine ran a major annual event for women in the community escaping domestic violence. Employees spoke of it with genuine pride. They owned the effort, both as individuals and as an organization. And this led to a powerful, shared sense of self-actualization.

Social Activism

Companies that tie their identity to valuable social causes win the loyalty of their workforces.

There are endless "causes" that can and should be part of the intentional creation of workplace cultures. Many corporate initiatives appeal broadly to commonly held values. These can be very effective. Even better is when individual team leaders develop meaningful relationships with the people reporting directly to them. If these managers can get to really know the people working with them, they can instill a new level of meaning. When managers know what makes their employees tick, they can connect with the organization to deep, personally held values. For example, if you have several people on your team who have a passion for yoga, could a once-a-week yoga class be facilitated? If someone is passionate about environmental causes, could they lead a project to reduce your department's environmental footprint?

Even some values that may seem hard to relate to your organization can be supported. For example, I had an employee that climbed mountains for fun. He had a wide-eyed, irrepressible sense of adventure. When we chatted, I'd show genuine interest in what trip he was preparing for. We talked about how the overtime he was working would fund equipment he would purchase. When he worked out in the office gym, I'd comment on the fitness he needed to get to the top of Kilimanjaro! It wasn't difficult to connect work (our business) with what was important to him.

The social activism piece does not mean blindly throwing your organization's hat into every highly politicized debate. Rather it is using discernment to identify causes that truly matter and striving to support them. On an individual level it is encouraging leaders to find out what causes matter to employees, and when appropriate, facilitating their ability to champion these causes.

Work must give us a sense of meaning and purpose. It must connect with our individual values. Our career is a huge part of our lives. Without creating this connection, we cannot be fully self-actualized.

The last several chapters gave concrete directions on how we can confidently meet the psychological needs of our people. And yet there's one more level of the building of psychological requirements that's especially high-leverage and, alas, will not apply to all your people. Let's examine what we call "positive energizers" in the next chapter.

ROOFTOP SELF-ACTUALIZATION TWO OF TWO—MEANING

Reflections:

1) In what ways does your organization appeal to your employees' personal values?
2) How do your personal values align with your organization's?
3) How can you support your people to find more meaning in their work?

Actions:

1)

2)

3)

Chapter 13

Lightning Rod
Cultivating Positive Energy

Imagine a workplace where nearly everyone is excited to be there.

People come in early and stay late, not because of a never-ending workload, but because work is exciting. Even though the volume of high value work is astonishing, burnout is unheard of. People volunteer without a sense of fear or obligation.

Work is fun.

It's important not to trivialize fun. Fun isn't some meaningless frivolity reserved for child's play. When work is engaging and meaningful it is fun. People volunteer to be a part of something fun. ("Volunteering" is the emotional tone of their labor.) Fun activities are punctuated with frequent celebrations, spontaneous creativity, and sustained periods of flow. Fun has a vibrational energy that's distinctly positive.

In the preceding chapters, I showed the workplace application of a hierarchy of psychological needs. Every great organization must intentionally cultivate a culture that meets these needs for their people to create motivated and loyal workforces. Businesses that actively attend to workers' needs have high morale and the benefits that flow from that. They're powerful and effective. But there is another level. Some organizations have a distinct energy, an almost *electric positivity* about them. Unfortunately, we rarely recognize this.

We're far more likely to see the negative energy.

Negative energy shows up in several ways. The most obvious is a violent workplace. People call each other names with four letter adjectives. This may not always be face to face, but there's a palpable animosity. Lots of absenteeism, especially on Mondays and Fridays, is a sign of a negative culture. Interdepartmental rivalries aren't based on healthy competition, but hostility between bunkered enemy lines. Poison personalities are well known and found across the organization. Finally, most negative cultures have massive distrust between frontline workers and senior management.

Does some of this sound too familiar?

Gallup provides a saddening glimpse into modern workplaces.[27] Throughout the world, only 13% of workers are engaged: genuinely emotionally committed to the workplace. 63% of employees are disengaged. And 24% are "actively disengaged," — they hate being at work. These workers make choices and engage in behaviors that sabotage the goals of their business.

What if this negativity disappeared? What if people were having fun? What if high productivity, innovation, and great teamwork were the norm?

At the top of a building, lightning strikes with an excess of 300 million volts. In all modern structures, this is perfectly safe. A tall steel rod sits atop every building. Lightning strikes this rod, which is deliberately the highest point on the structure. It directs the energy from a strike down the steel rod, through a cable, and safely into the ground. Through architectural design, that energy is directed. As in nature, can human spirit—emotional energy—be directed for the business' use? In short, yes. Some rare workplaces have abundant, seemingly inexplicable positive energy.

---

[27] Gallup 2013 — The referenced study reflects a worldwide survey. Readers in North America might find some satisfaction in knowing the percentage of actively engaged employees is higher in Canada and the USA, but overall, it is still a tragic fact that most workers are not engaged.

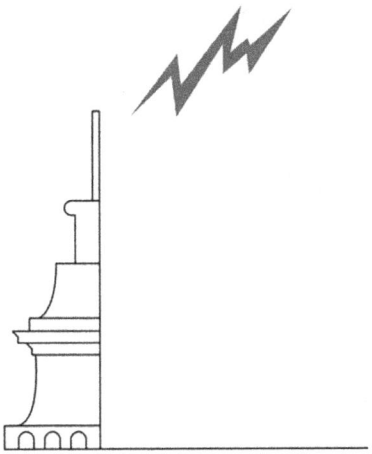

Positive Energizers

Positive Energizers are real. They are the subject of much academic research. And you intuitively know them when you see them.

These are the people we are naturally attracted to. They are open and welcoming. They offer support and are genuinely happy to roll up their sleeves to help problem-solve. They bring joy and friendliness to most conversations. We seek them out when we want to be uplifted: they genuinely create good energy, in stark contrast to people who drain your energy. We feel more vital and enthusiastic in their company.

Academics[28] observe that positive energizers are virtuous — they are genuinely good people. They are quick to forgive others and readily admit to their own shortcomings. They are trustworthy. They

---

[28] Kim Cameron is the foremost researcher of Positive Energizers in workplaces. His work has informed a great deal of this chapter. Notable books by Kim Cameron include *Positively Energizing Leadership* and *Practicing Positive Leadership*. I recommend them both.

haven't got an "agenda". They give of themselves generously and without need for payback or reward.

We might think they will be recognized in a meeting as the most extroverted and outwardly cheerful personalities. But actually, extroversion is not predictive of positive energizers. They are not domineering or self-aggrandizing. Introverts can be just as energizing as extroverts. We all know people who are thoughtful, and sometimes a bit reserved. Yet when they do speak up, they have a sincerity coupled with grounded optimism that elevates the discussion.

Positive energizers can be identified by a common set of learnable attributes:

- Volunteer to help
- Express gratitude and humility
- Instill confidence and empower others
- Smile a lot
- Forgive readily and see mistakes as learning opportunities
- Create personal connections by showing genuine interest in others
- Give credit to others for their contributions
- Use active listening and are empathetic
- Tend to find the bigger meaning in things: they inspire others
- Their default is to trust others
- Set high performance standards

Given these simple, yet relatively rare characteristics it is not hard to see why we want to find and elevate these people. They have way oversized impact on teams. In fact, their contribution far exceeds their structural, hierarchical authority. Research by Wayne Baker shows that the degree to which a person brings positive energy is "significantly more important in predicting performance than a person's position in the information or influence [hierarchy]."[29]

These people have relational energy that fundamentally changes the work dynamic among colleagues. In their presence, you will find better individual job performance. People will report higher job satisfaction and engagement.

Positive energy includes fun, but it's much more than that. Positive energy is a cultural attribute we can nurture. Let's explore the following features of a positive culture that we can deliberately nurture to create space for positive energizers to emerge and thrive.

1. friendly, quality interpersonal relationships
2. strong, steady leadership
3. focus on the mission — alignment
4. task enabling
5. flow

Let's examine each of these qualities in a little more detail.

One) **Friendly, quality interpersonal relationships**

It's surprising how often in my consulting work I find senior leaders that don't see their own destructive interpersonal environments. Workers are gruff with one another. Many leaders are paternalistic and arrogant. What passes as light-hearted criticism is often plain old disrespect. A bullying boss is all too common. Overly aggressive, competitive posturing is everywhere. And, far too often, leadership behaviors are overtly racist and/or sexist.

Positive work cultures have a friendly tone and leaders that model kindness. People greet each other with warmth and respect. They're inclusive—everyone's contribution is valued, and all voices are welcome. Listening is valued and practiced. When relationships

---
[29] Page 37, *Positively Energizing Leadership* by Kim Cameron.

are warm and encouraging, the inherent social safety leads to creative and cooperative problem solving.

Two) **Strong, steady leadership**

Truly embodying and consistently modeling positivity is essential. We'll talk a lot more about this in Part Three. **Strong** and **steady** leadership is still required. Being friendly and positive can be mistakenly seen as being soft and tolerant of mediocrity. The opposite is true. Strong leaders set high standards because they sincerely believe in their people's potential. Constantly playing musical chairs among your leaders leads to instability and the tenuous management of the emotional context of the workplace. Consciously creating a positive culture requires long-term commitment. Steady guidance is critical.

Great leaders often aren't high-profile, gregarious extroverts. Consider business author Jim Collins' observation: transformational leaders are most often shy, self-effacing, and reserved. Yet they are very ambitious for the success of the organization. They set high standards and have a clear vision that stands the test of time.

Three) **Focus on the mission**

The larger the organization, the more likely it is to be segmented, departmentalized, siloed, and divided. This drives layers of bureaucracy. Do the people in the IT department feel connected to the production team? Does the accounting team know what drives the sales cycle? Rarely!

Does every department know the BIG goals? If there aren't metrics for job performance that directly relate to the company's mission, then it will be impossible—from a cultural perspective—to create a workplace committed to a mission that unites everyone. All employees working for an organization should be able to talk about their company's end users. Who buys the product/service and why? This common reference point makes a singular culture possible.

Four) **Task Enabling**

High energy organizations know how to get stuff done. The most productive businesses do everything possible to help individual workers and teams have the resources necessary to accomplish their goals. This requires a broad and continuous sharing of resources—money, information, expert advice, and more.

Task enabling leaders to have positive regards for their employees. They value the work people do and ensure they're reducing barriers to productivity. When done right, these leaders build efficacy in their team members. Their staff not only work productively but also believe in their personal power to achieve results. They take on an identity of achieving.

Five) **Flow**

People want to be happy at work. In fact, quality research shows that most people have more happy moments at work relative to their home lives. This is because so much of our personal lives lack flow: think TV-watching, social media scrolling, and scurrying around with chores, childcare, and other must-dos.

People want to be engaged and productive. We intuitively know that heightened periods of performance are exhilarating—being in states of flow or "in the zone" is profoundly satisfying. This flow state has recognizable features that can be intentionally designed:[30]

- clear goals
- near term measures of achievement with immediate, automatic feedback
- adequate challenge to draw out intensity without being overwhelmingly difficult

---

[30] Mihaly Czientmihaly's pioneering book *Flow: The Psychology of Optimal Experience*."

- an environment that doesn't constantly distract
- feelings of autonomy and control over one's own work

When flow is present for an individual, action and consciousness blend. Time disappears, enabling sustained focus. This state of timeless, focused achievement is bliss!

These characteristics of flow can be true in nearly any undertaking. When done in a social setting, organic moments of celebration arise. Achievement is recognized.

Every line supervisor can learn the simple ingredients found in states of flow. They can focus on building the conditions of flow into the work of their subordinates.

The upcoming Part Three of this book will give many more insights into creating positive energy through recognizing and nurturing *positive energizers*. You have people right now in your workplaces that are already making a big, beneficial impact on your culture. If you're like most people, you may have a hard time identifying them and seeing just what a substantial difference they make. In Chapter 16, I'll provide a simple, accurate way for you to identify them and the de-energizers.

Through the last several chapters, we've examined the varied and hierarchical psychological needs of every workplace. Most businesses fail to meet them. This is often true because most leaders and HR departments are simply unaware of these emotional components of people's psyches. It's not a conspiracy or evil plot to make workers suffer, but simply an absence of active management towards the creation of a flourishing organization.

You now have a framework for creating a strong and effective workplace. It must be attended to with deliberate intention and ongoing management.

Reflections:

1) What is the emotional tone of leadership in your organization?
2) How does your organization get all employees on the same page—focused on one mission?
3) Does your work result in flow states of productivity and enjoyment? How about the work of your team or employees?
4) What's fun about work? How could you have more fun?

Actions:

1)

2)

3)

PART III

ENGINEERING WORKPLACE CULTURE:

THEORY TO ACTION

Chapter 14

Designing Cultural Rhythm and Accountability

How it is that the people of Armenia have maintained a visceral conflict with the people of Azerbaijan for *over 800 years*? Why is Sicily associated with organized crime after decades of international police efforts to root it out? Are your friends still cheering for the hometown team they passionately rooted for when they were kids? Why is it for some people Coke (not Pepsi) is "it"? How is it that Amazon has such a pervasive history of poor labor relations that staff openly complain about their employer, <u>even</u> while doing their jobs?

All these long-standing traits are cultural. Accidental cultural artifacts are often so well established that they're scarcely mentioned, except occasionally by people on the outside looking in. For the people who are living these cultural traits daily, they go unnoticed. They're unremarkable. It's just the way it is. It's so pervasive and consistent that it's like a fish in water. The fish never thinks "Oh cool! I live in water." The fish only thinks about water when it is forcefully taken out of water. Just like you. If we removed the air from the room you're sitting in, suddenly air would be extraordinarily important. In the meantime, you don't think about air.

Culture is like that. Most workplaces have cultures without deliberate intention. Certainly, employers have turned their minds to working conditions, pay and benefits, and similar things. But how many have aspired to grow a very specific, well-articulated culture? Almost none. Has your company got a clear, well-defined cultural intention?

DESIGNING CULTURAL RHYTHM AND ACCOUNTABILITY

Culture must be designed.

Leaders often overlook that culture ought to be intentionally crafted. Sadly, a lot of organizations awaken to their culture one day only to realize it's flawed or downright toxic. They realize no one was directing the culture as the firm grew over the last five, ten, twenty, or sometimes hundreds of years.

Like any other aspect of an organization: pay and benefits, operational processes, customer service, marketing, etc., culture ought to be deliberately crafted.

Let's remember how we defined culture earlier in the book. Culture lives among the frontline personnel. It's their beliefs, feelings, and perceived shared history that shape the way employees perform operations on a day-to-day basis. It's a mood, a vibe, and a way of being. It shows up in everyday ways people speak to one another, how they dress, and how they act. It's pervasive and consistent. Of course, some people don't conform to the "norms" of a culture, and the degree to which that's true is <u>also</u> culture.

Obviously, culture isn't as linear, mechanical, or quantitative as other business areas. But it's just as strategic and, arguably, has higher impact. Therefore, intentional culture management is essential. Just like other vital aspects of your business, building an ideal culture will take time. But the bottom line is that culture isn't fundamentally different from, or less important than, other key organizational elements.

Cultures can be built. Cultures can be changed for the better.

So how do you do this? There are two major themes running throughout our discussion of cultural change. These are (1) what we call "cultural rhythm," and (2) measurement and accountability.

The term cultural rhythm refers to how culture permeates an organization. We build culture from the bottom up, even if the cultural vision ought to come from the top. Therefore, senior leaders must understand that frontline workers and supervisors own the culture.

To successfully change culture, you must ensure norms, vision, and strategy flow from senior leadership all the way to the frontline. Senior leadership crafts the strategy and vision for the culture, but they must ensure it is disseminated to the supervisors and frontline workers. Then, feedback and effectiveness measures are passed back "up" the organization, creating a dynamic flow of continued cultural evolution. Think of leadership as the heart that pumps blood through the arteries (internal communications) to the hands and feet that do the work. This flow is the cultural lifeblood of an organization.

As you craft changes that will permeate the organization, you must go beyond a simple mission and vision statement. You must include specificity and rigor. Definite tasks and standards that support cultural change. You must have individually mandated leaders who are accountable for cultivating these changes in the workforce psyche.

Peter Drucker famously said, "what gets measured gets managed." The essence of effective management is measurement. Culture may seem slippery and qualitative (and in some ways, it is), but it's certainly not beyond quantitative rigor.

Let's consider one of the first organizations I worked with on a specific cultural change initiative. It was a prison facing near catastrophic challenges. Labor relations were so bad that every day, the most basic organizational tasks, like whether the prisoners would be fed, housed in the right cells, and released on the correct date, were in peril. Then there were the worries causing senior leaders to lose sleep at night. The fear was they'd lose control of the prison. Frontline staff wouldn't do what they needed to in the event of an uprising. If inmates acted up, would lackluster, uncommitted staff fail to react? Would some insignificant event lead to a riot, massive property damage, hostages, lost lives, and a tragic, permanent failure?

The start of my work with this prison began following an "incident" I won't disclose. It led to the sudden firing of the warden

DESIGNING CULTURAL RHYTHM AND ACCOUNTABILITY

and his right hand, most senior subordinate. The organization was in crisis, they knew it, and it was an inflection point where they wanted to act. They simply didn't know how to start.

After various briefings and observation, I sat down with the senior executive team to begin a cultural transformation. After summarizing the process, we created a set of measurables specific to their behaviors. For example, every day, leaders start the day with a formal act of appreciation for a colleague. Think back to the chapter on self-esteem and the discussion of "real recognition." This isn't a just a "thank you," but an act of deeply witnessing the accomplishment of a peer, superior, or subordinate.

To hold leaders accountable, we assigned them accountability partners who they checked in with each day. Most leaders blind copied their accountability partners on their daily appreciation emails.

After the training rolled out to all levels of leadership, every single day started with supervisors at all levels giving, and often receiving, gratitude. Take a moment to imagine the ripple effect this had on an organization's culture. In very little time, there was a palpable difference in the prison's energy. The first time I set foot in the prison complex, the heavy, oppressive energy hit me squarely in the chest. The place was tight, unhappy, and on edge. Six months after the culture change project began, people greeted me warmly as I entered the building. The tone and tenor of management meetings had good-natured laughter and camaraderie. You didn't need to be an empathy expert to feel the stark change. A growth of positive energy had taken root. The men and women who worked there felt it, too, and that encouraged further cultural change.

From the outset, this prison had many habits so well ingrained that no one in leadership saw them as caustic barriers to success. For example, they always hired new corrections officers as auxiliaries before being considered for full-time positions. They'd often hang around for months, or even years, before receiving an opportunity to transition to full-time, permanent employment.

Staff, including executive leaders, used the term "JAFA." I heard it repeatedly. They'd say things like "assign it to a JAFA," or "a JAFA can do this or that." I realized it was an acronym for a certain role.

So, one day I asked, "what specific role does JAFA refer to?"

Those in the room looked around at each other and chuckled. They explained it was slang for the auxiliaries.

"Well, how are they any different from other corrections officers?" I asked.

The reply was, "We refer to the auxiliaries as JAFAs because it stands for"—and I quote — "just another f***ing auxiliary."

And they'd refer to them in person as such. This sort of degrading style of humor and underlying resentment permeated the cultural environment. They described other divisions and teams in similar terms (viz. "those f***ing a**holes in the control room"). This macho culture saw these habits as harmless.

While this may seem somewhat trivial, it sets the tone for communication. And it had a profound impact on the effectiveness of the organization.

So, how did we check this behavior in a measurable, strategic way?

We gathered senior leadership, and, after much discussion, we created a formal policy: they would fine managers for using those terms. There were specific leaders responsible for ensuring the policy was enforced. It wasn't a huge fine, something like $50, but it eliminated those abusive behaviors almost overnight.

Consider what impact these two minor examples of change made for frontline staff. (There were, of course, many more). What would it feel like if you were previously called "JAFA" and are now referred to as "Officer?" Imagine, if you typically got no feedback and if you did, it was negative. Subtly, over a few months, you got meaningful recognition for the role you've played, referencing specific things you did that helped the organization meet its key objectives. You realize you and others are simply, and consistently, addressed respectfully and getting timely feedback on work well done.

The likelihood of executing a behavior or process change increases exponentially once a <u>specific</u> standard of measure is applied to hold individuals accountable. Further, specific leaders must commit to being held responsible for following through on the cultural change efforts.

Cultural change begins with translating the cultural vision into specific, measurable behaviors or outcomes that are used to create accountability. This vision, crafted by senior leadership, then flows through internal communications to all levels of the organization where it's owned by the shared experiences, norms, and behaviors of the frontline workers and supervisors.

In the next chapter, we examine how to gauge where your culture is. What's working? What needs changing? You're unlikely to navigate to a new place smoothly if your organization can't find itself on the map.

Reflections:

1) What needs to change in your organization's cultural rhythm? What are a few measurable behaviors, processes, or outcomes that you could change or implement to make your cultural change real? (These may become actions).
2) Which individuals in your organization can serve as "project managers" for cultural change to ensure organizational accountability?

3) How well does the cultural vision "flow" from senior leadership to the frontline? Are there any blockages (barriers that need identification and active management)?

Actions:

1)

2)

3)

Chapter 15

Establishing Baseline Measures

At the time of writing, I am fifty-four years old. I eat well. I play hockey. I don't have any scary habits, like smoking or drinking in excess. I think I'm healthy. Yet my doctor still insists on an annual checkup. He requires blood work, I pee in a bottle, and he does a physical exam. Mostly, there's nothing much worth talking about, but last year he recommended I take a B12 supplement, because I'm eating fewer animal products. It feels ordinary. Simple. You probably agree this is standard practice. You probably also agree this practice makes sense and is worth doing.

There's an exact parallel to doing a cultural audit in your workplace. Everything might be fine. You may need a tweak to one small thing or another. Or there might be a cancerous tumor that because you looked, you find it, remove it, and restore health!

This chapter focuses on establishing baseline measures for the cultural health of your organization. I'll share a free framework you can implement to calculate your cultural energy score and identify the key contributors to effective culture within your organization immediately.

Please note that for large, complex organizations, you can outsource this process to a specialized firm. When my firm (www.HappinessMeansBusiness.com) assists our clients, we have ready-to-go survey instruments and assessment protocols that quickly provide a comprehensive assessment. You may delegate this to a senior leader in human resources, or to a project manager responsible for driving this culture change project. In either case, you'll want to focus on receiving the following two outcomes: 1) a clear picture of your cultural health, and 2) how each key leader contributes to it.

ESTABLISHING BASELINE MEASURES

A common hurdle in collecting measures relating to culture is that the process often isn't as lean as we'd like—there's cumbersome formality. When organizations set out to gather these measures, it becomes a massive undertaking with employees slogging through 100-item questionnaires. Further, frontline workers in organizations often see the formality around this process as an opportunity to send a message to management. Sweeping employee satisfaction surveys and comprehensive assessments are often distorted by underlying politics. This is particularly true in unionized environments. For example, when a once-a-year formal survey is about to be distributed, word gets around about what grievances need airing. The workforce takes on a bit of groupthink.

We recommend a "quick and dirty" approach with an emphasis on speed and flexibility. The goal is to get an accurate snapshot of the workforce's mood as efficiently as possible. A handful of thoughtful questions and/or observations often provide as much insight as a more formal institutional assessment, but with much less friction.

We value the idea of quantifying the amount of good energy being generated in an organization. Here's a simple, lean, and effective framework we created. This resource created by University of Michigan Professor Kim is available with instructions at: http://www.HappinessMeansBusiness.com/BPP.

This framework combines principles from the most influential literature on organizational psychology and leadership. We intentionally use the work of Dr. Cameron for his pioneering work on energy networks within organizations.

After years of empirical studies, he observes: "The display of positive energy in leaders, in fact, has proved much more important in predicting performance than the amount of information or influence a leader possesses."[31]

---

[31] Kim Cameron in *Positively Energizing Leadership* (2021), page 54.

Wouldn't you like to know in a factual, statistically accurate way who among your leaders is a lightning rod of positivity energy?

The framework provided at the link above will allow you to determine the overall energy score of your organization quickly and identify your greatest energy contributors and those most in need of improvement.

A key step for establishing baseline measures is to understand where positive energy comes from in a workplace. We can determine where individuals go when they need help and how energized they feel when engaging with other employees. Identifying these two patterns will serve as an excellent map of positive energy sources.

I believe that line employees ought to go to their supervisor when they need help. Yet, we all know that frequently doesn't happen.

I recall distinctly an absurd reality from early in my career. I worked alongside a manager who oversaw a team of people doing the same work as my direct reports. This other manager and I had side-by-side offices. He observed one day how my staff would often queue outside my door, particularly in the late afternoon when they were confident I wrapped up my meetings for the day up. He scoffed and said, "You've made your people dependent on you!"

I was a bit taken aback at first. Was I doing something wrong? Later, as I drove home from work, I realized he didn't have his staff lining up outside his door. In fact, I'd rarely see any of his staff approach his door, ever. He had a prickly, difficult communication style. His staff would simply sooner be struggling with their complex projects than go to him for help. He managed data, assigned processes, and passed judgment on performance. Whereas I relished being in the trenches with my people; teaming up with them to win.

Have you ever had a leader you hesitated to talk to? You maybe even dreaded interacting with them. Your experience was negative in multiple ways. Your supervisor was perhaps condescending or critical. They had negative energy about the organization, your colleagues, clients, or their personal lives. They were low energy, uninspired and "putting in time." After you chatted, even if you got the answers you needed, you felt drained. Your own outlook was diminished. These *de-energizers* suck the life out of your culture.

In contrast, positive energizers are the people you want to see. They're upbeat, they like what they do, and they're generally happy to help. Most organizations don't recognize how frequently these people are unofficial (non-supervisory) supporters of their colleagues. After getting the help you need, you feel happy and inspired to put the knowledge you just gained to use. These are the people you need to find and elevate.

Kim Cameron often uses a slightly altered John Quincy Adams quote that makes this simple observation:

> *If your actions inspire others to dream more, learn more, do more, and become more, you are a positively energizing leader!*

To figure out who these people are and what the general state of your culture is, begin with a simple survey that asks two questions about each member of your organization (or your team, department, or division). You want to know 1) where energy comes from vs. where it's taken away, and 2) where people go for support. The survey asks each member in a group:

- Please respond with a number from (1) very de-energized to (5) very energized. When I interact with Steve Smith, I feel…
- Please respond with a number from (1) very unlikely to (5) very likely. When I need help, I would go to Steve Smith for support…

By plugging the survey results into this framework, you'll receive the output. Here's an example of a fictional organization with twenty key team members.

Organization Score   *2.70*

Energy Contribution (1-5)

Sara Kimson, Hourly	4.10
Margaret Smith, Director	4.05
Leroy Bennett, Senior VP	3.85
Sady Sanders, Hourly	3.80
Chase Henry, Director	3.50
Josh Thompson, Senior VP	3.30
Joe Grant, Hourly	3.05
Luke Davis, VP	2.90
Travis Jones, CMO	2.85
Sean Jong, Hourly	2.65
Mitch Gay, Analyst	2.60
Roy Rodney, Hourly	2.15
Gretta Henderson, Assistant	1.95
Brady Daniels, CFO	1.95
Ron Davidson, CEO	1.95
David Kelly, Hourly	1.95
Mei Zoro, Hourly	1.90
Tammy Cooper, Director	1.90
Ben Tatum, VP	1.85
Cindy Bennet, HR Manager	1.75

ESTABLISHING BASELINE MEASURES

In this example, you can quickly see which of the leaders are solving other people's problems and juicing them up. Not only are the leaders at the top of the list strategic thinking partners, but they're inspiring others around them. At the other end of the spectrum, you can see people who, frankly, your frontline needs to be protected from. The overall organizational score of 2.70 shows there's a lot of opportunity for improvement. Imagine the vast cultural difference there'd be if they could move that corporate score to 4 or higher. Productivity would soar!

Of course, a culture of positive energy is ideal, but just how important is it? According to researchers Spreitzer, Lam and Quinn "positively energized people are more adaptive, more creative, suffer from fewer physical illnesses and accidents, and experience richer interpersonal relationships than others."[32] It's been shown that positive energizing individuals aren't only higher performing themselves, but also elevate others' performance.[33] Finally, Kim Cameron reminds us that "the scientific research is clear:... positive energy is, by a large margin, a more significant factor in the performance of individuals and organizations than people's titles, the information they possess, the influence they exert, or their personality attributes." It's worth reading that last quote again!

You may think about cultural health as a "net charge" on a spectrum from highly negative to highly positive. Each person acts as a node in this network, contributing his or her energizing or de-energizing effect to the overall culture. An important note here is that positive energizers aren't necessarily the most extraverted,

---

[32] Spreitzer, Lam & Quinn "Building a Sustainable Model of Human Energy in Organizations: Exploring the Critical Role of Resources" published in *The Academy of Management Annals.*

[33] Baker, Cross & Wooten "Positive organizational network analysis and energizing relationships" in *Positive organizational scholarship: Foundations of a new discipline.*

outgoing, or "peppy." In fact, there's little to no correlation between how one is assessed as an energizer and how one scores on personality tests for extroversion. Their energizing effect has everything to do with how they support and engage with other employees.

Individualizing these sources of good culture is important, as opposed to having a catchall assessment of the organization. That's because overall assessments don't give us insight into the firm's cultural leaders. So, there's little guidance for immediately generating more positive energy and driving cultural transformation.

In this approach, you can identify the net energy creators and consider how to leverage them for positive cultural change. Of equal importance, it helps organizations identify leaders who correspond to a net energy deficit—those who are toxic to the firm's culture. These are leaders who staff simply don't like. In our experience, most organizations have measures associated with poor performance in task execution. But they rarely have a good feel for identifying cultural de-energizers or processes to deal with them appropriately.

Having established these baseline measures for an organization's overall cultural health and the energy contribution of each leader, you'll have built a strong, quantitative foundation for cultural transformation. When my company performs culture audits for our clients, we also conduct a representative sample of in-depth interviews with people at all levels within an organization's hierarchy. This qualitative analysis informs how we implement an overarching culture-change project.

Is all this talk of "positivity" just a bunch of wishful, all-too-sweet sentiments? If we get too positive, won't our standards swirl to ridiculously low levels so everyone can feel good all the time? That's the question we turn to in the next chapter.

ESTABLISHING BASELINE MEASURES

Reflections:

1) How might you gather baselines measures? Will you drive this, delegate it, or outsource it?
2) At a glance, how do you think key leaders in your organization contribute to the "net charge" of the firm's energy level? How do you contribute to it?
3) In what ways does positive energy matter to you and your people?

Actions:

1) Explore our cultural health assessment framework and apply it to your organization. This resource is available for free at www.HappinessMeansbusiness.com/BPP.
2)

3)

Chapter 16

Positive Paradigm

Just after my fifteenth birthday, after years of having newspaper routes, a nearby service station hired me on as a gas jockey. Back then, all gas stations were full serve. The service station was almost entirely about gas sales, with a tiny interior store that sold chips, pop, and chocolate bars.

The owner was rarely there. It was a simple business to run. Pump gas, take money, repeat. Training a new employee comprised teaming them up with someone who had more than a few days experience. When the boss did pop in, he'd cheerily say a few words, order one of his staff to dip the tanks (see how much fuel the station had) and take off. On his way out the door, he'd grab a Mars chocolate bar, a Coke, and yell over his shoulder, "I'll pay later."

What do you think all his employees did as we waited around for cars and trucks to drive in? We ate junk food and said to each other, "I'll pay later."

When I first worked there, I thought the statement, "I'll pay later" meant something. However, once I'd been around long enough to gain the trust of other employees, it became apparent that the statement was a joke. Everyone, me included, stole from our boss every shift. I'm ashamed of it even now, and I didn't really like it then, either. I quit shortly after I started because the *culture* of the workplace rubbed me the wrong way, although I wouldn't have known to call it culture then. I just didn't want to be someplace where stealing was the norm.

Here's the thing: who sets the standard? Of course, it was the owner. He modeled eating Mars bars and drinking Coke was something you do for "free." I get it intellectually: the junk food *he* ate came out of *his* margins. He had the right to take stuff from the inventory *he* paid for. The rest of us were stealing.

It's essential to set high standards. Moreover, it's essential that leaders, at all levels, continuously model those standards. To understand this, let's explore what I call the Positive Paradigm.

Let's begin by establishing what applying positive psychology in workplace settings is *not*: it's not just positive thinking, it's not pop psychology self-help, it's not patting everyone on the back, and it's not endless sunshine and rainbows.

It's the science of human flourishing applied to organizations. It's real, genuine, and proven.

Positive leadership is well-developed work based on positive psychology research. Kim Cameron, the previously mentioned leading academic, says, "far from mitigating against hard work, or representing soft, simple, and syrupy actions, the strategies require effort, elevated standards, and genuine competence."

Consider what most big organizations do. They set process prescriptions for frontline workers that are readily achievable for most, if not all, employees. Managers do this, often subconsciously, because managing poor performers is hard. And confronting lousy work is perceived as a fast path to low popularity among direct reports. So, managers look at a process and say, "what's the minimum everybody can do?" then they prescribe a method that employees follow to meet this minimal level of effectiveness.

That has a counterproductive effect: everybody gets over the low bar, but all the workers capable of doing better work (which is most of them) only aspire to the low standard set by management. They mistakenly believe that low levels of work are, in fact, completely appropriate work because that's the standard being set.

You may see how this is backward. Instead, you can set standards based on what top performers do and say - "This is what great work looks like," then move people toward that. You'll see far greater outcomes than you thought possible and drive a culture of continuous improvement.

Several years ago, I had oversight of large teams of disability case managers (and their managers). Prior to my involvement in what I'll call case management best practices, our firm had minimal performance standards. Case managers followed generic policies set by senior management. Outcomes from staff were all over the map, and the organization wasn't well-liked by our clients.

I worked with the managers to set more aspirational standards. For instance, "Every file must have a complete written plan in place showing the history of the worker's injury, their personal circumstances, treatment, and return-to-work plan." In the beginning, we intentionally left a lot of the details around that standard blank. Eventually, through continuous learning, this standard grew more defined. In relatively little time, we saw examples of truly exceptional case planning. We publicly lauded these examples, created evaluations systems for measuring quality work, and bit-by-bit filled in details of what excellence looked like.

Some ambiguity is okay—what matters is that we raised the bar. Instead of generic policies, we agreed that anybody should be able to read the case management plan and completely understand our collective mission regarding a specific client and their individual circumstances. We didn't prescribe activity. We looked for indicators of a plan that will succeed. That's a bit more of an inspiring standard, isn't it?

Similarly, we set customer service standards that simply said, "we're going to survey 5% percent of our clients (injured workers) and ask them how satisfied they are with their case manager's work." We knew from historical data that case managers typically averaged a rating of just 6 on a 1 to 10 scale.

Our new, regular surveying quickly identified outliers of consistently high performance. We saw some case managers averaging 9/10. This was remarkable, given that the role was to make difficult legal decisions that deeply affected clients in the most vulnerable of times. Pain and an uncertain injury outcome were the overlay in our clients' already complex lives.

By looking at the best among us, we knew what was doable. We set a standard of 8.5. A consensus quickly emerged among the case managers that the standard was simply way too high. But we set it anyway. And all we did was keep pointing out the examples of case managers who were meeting or exceeding it.

We publicized their extraordinary performance. We logged what they did, shared anonymous examples of their work, and provided some basic blueprints for how they did so well. Others caught on. Not only did they realize it was doable, but they also felt like a part of a more competitive environment where they could point to these outstanding performers and say, "I want to be in that number!"

Within a few months, the culture of the case management division changed and in a little less than two years, it was totally transformed. Our clients' recovery and return to work were hugely improved, and they were genuinely grateful for our service!

This is a real-world illustration of what researchers sometimes call positive deviance and what I call the Positive Paradigm.

Organizational leaders focus on negative outliers. They spend most of their time dealing with problems or trying to move poor performers to baseline or normal. The Positive Paradigm flips that on its head. It says you should focus your time and attention on getting individuals to be outstanding.

Go from looking at poor performers and asking, "how can I fix them?" to looking at the best performers and asking, "how can I get more like them?"

This illustration contrasts the different ways of thinking...

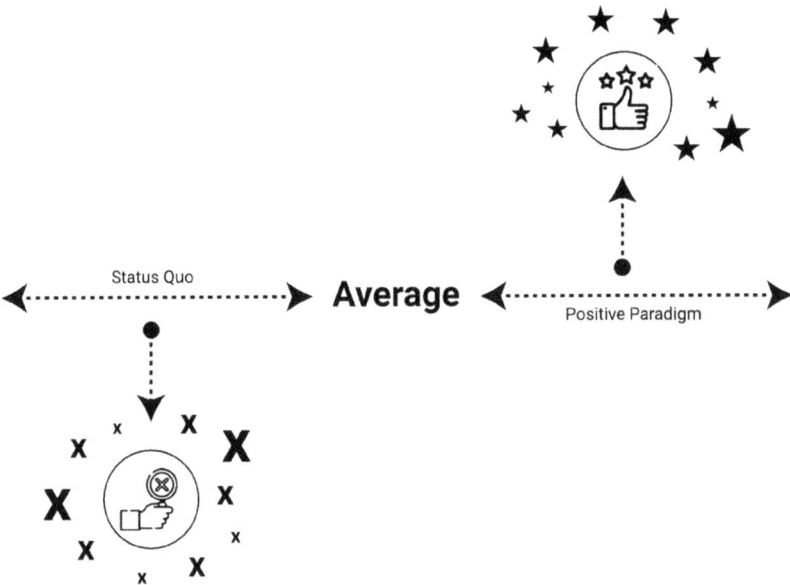

This doesn't mean you don't solve problems or don't acknowledge issues. Rather, you change your orientation to include the full spectrum of performance. You consider where your people excel, not just where they struggle. You consider what's going right, not just what's going wrong. And critically, you consider how your people can be extraordinary, not just effective.

This is a crucial understanding because, in traditional business leadership, mediocrity is the status quo (especially in larger, more bureaucratic businesses).

Why is that? Most organizations' leadership focuses on reducing variance. They create policies, processes, strategies, and structures intended to reduce deviance and eliminate outliers. If you picture a distribution of likely outcomes centered on the average, you'll find traditional business success at the center in the realm of standard operating procedure and meeting "acceptable" expectations.

POSITIVE PARADIGM

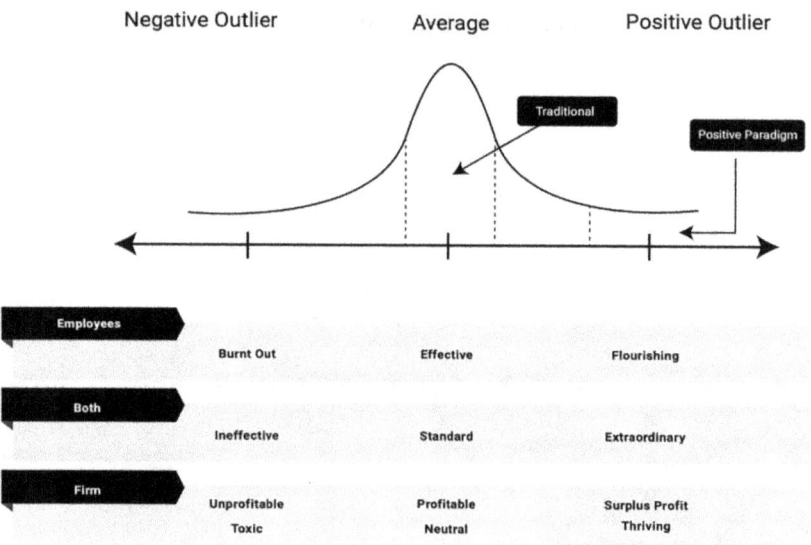

The positive paradigm isn't just concerned with ordinary success (productivity and profit). It's concerned with the extraordinary for individuals and organizations. This paradigm shift begins with how you set standards. If you keep aiming for mediocrity, you'll surely continue to hit the mark. Instead, you must continue to raise the bar. You must make extraordinary the new ordinary in your organization.

So, how do we move toward these higher, more inspiring standards? We read on!

Reflections:

1) How do you set standards in your organization?
2) What employees or teams in your organization come to mind as standards of exceptional work? How can individuals or business units model their performance?

Actions:

1)

2)

3)

Chapter 17

Appreciative Inquiry

I do a lot of keynote speaking at conferences and corporate events. Almost always, I begin my talks with the profound teaching that *happiness precedes success*. The standard social conditioning is the opposite; we're routinely taught success precedes happiness. We strive to accomplish, achieve, and gain *so* we can *then* be happy. This is simply wrong. And science convincingly agrees.

Happier individuals are more engaged, creative, and effective.[34] They're also better at solving problems. This pattern exists on an organizational level as well. In her book *Make More Money by Making Your Employees Happy*, Dr. Noelle Nelson cites that companies that appreciate employee value, enjoy returns more than triple those of firms that don't. The stock prices of the Fortune's "100 Best Companies to Work For" rose an average of 14% per year from 1998–2005, compared to 6% for the overall market.[35]

This is an observation where intuition, experience, and science converge. Happier workers are more effective workers.

What's more, recall that in the beginning of the book we discussed that happiness, understood as an abundance of positive emotions, leads to personal characteristics that are desirable in employees. Happy people are more sociable, intelligent, perceptive, and physically healthy. Not to mention they're more successful in marriage, friendship, and earning income.[36]

---

[34] Shawn Achor's The Happiness Advantage.
[35] Noelle Nelson's Make More Money by Making Your Employees Happy.
[36] Lyubomirsky S, King L, Diener E. The benefits of frequent positive affect: Does happiness lead to success? Psychol Bull. 2005.

If you want to cultivate workplaces where employees are happier and more effective, you must design meetings and projects to facilitate positive emotions as part of the business process.

In this chapter, we'll examine an effective, well-validated business improvement method. Appreciative Inquiry. It's designed to motivate individuals to bring their best selves to problem-solving. It does this so well because it's strengths-based, positively oriented, and encourages employees to set high standards.

Appreciative Inquiry starts from a "what's working" mindset. It formally inventories assets already contributing to current success, and it's grounded in current business realities.

The model begins with defining the problem and includes five components.

1. Define

The key to this step is to frame and define the problem from a perspective that encourages the imagination of those solving the problem. In a standard business meeting, problems are framed narrowly: "Hey everyone, we called this meeting because our quality control isn't working well. We have 10% defects on the factory line." This is a typical reference to a typical agenda item. Wouldn't you agree we could accurately rename most agendas "list of problems"? The framing of the discussion immediately narrows individuals' perspectives. It gets them thinking to fix what's wrong and it anchors them to the status quo (in this example, 10%).

Imagine beginning the meeting this way: "Hey everyone, this is a brainstorming meeting where we want to channel your creativity to look at the best possible quality control outcomes we could generate…" Framing the situation in a positive way (e.g., what's the best we might do), stimulates creativity and enthusiasm. It also gets people thinking in terms of how to be exceptional (remember the

Positive Paradigm from earlier) as opposed to bringing 10% back to baseline.

The model begins with an expansive definition of the subject to be discussed, intended to spark creativity and ambition.

2. Discover

This phase includes taking inventory of what's working and what assets are available within the organization. In short, what are the organization's strengths and what resources can be brought to bear? This requires searching beyond what's currently deployed to solve the problem. In thinking about these resources, it's often helpful to create a framework, such as a fishbone chart, to structure the organization's assets.

The idea is to examine the organization's situation rigorously. In doing so, leaders stretch beyond the limited scope of the problem and consider the capability of the organization. See the illustration:

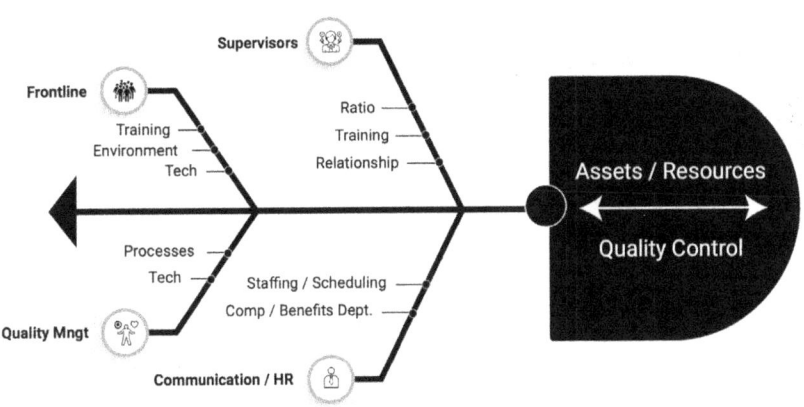

3. Dream

This step is all about defining and articulating the ideal vision for the outcome of the project or resolving the problem. As implied by the word "dream," this vision should be aspirational (e.g., best possible outcome) as opposed to incremental. And it should be longer term (it won't happen tomorrow). Although it's important to note that even an aspirational goal should include achievable, incremental steps.

In the dream step, leaders should be idealistic, but still specific and concrete. What's the ideal vision for productivity, for staffing, for quality control? And so on.

4. Design

In the design phase, you take the assets identified in the discovery phase and align them with the vision articulated in the dream phase. What collaborative and strategic processes can you leverage to move the organization toward that shared, long-term vision? Echoing the cautionary note in the dream step—this is where leadership makes the aspirational goal incremental and tangible. Thinking here should be done with an eye toward implementation and shorter time horizons.

Designs get practical. It's about what's achievable. Indeed, it may become very incremental, so measures of some progress are assured. It's about direction and long-term vision, while maintaining effectiveness in the near term.

5. Destiny

This phase is all about implementation and execution. A key success factor for this phase is avoiding the top-down dynamic. What often happens is employees do some exploratory work on a matter, then it gets taken to the executive team or board of directors where a final decision is made regarding the model or strategy the organization will use. This often stifles creativity and doesn't allow for people to play or experiment with novel ways to make improvements.

Ideally, senior leadership will encourage autonomous action (think bottom-up). This could mean approving more pilot projects or even pilot projects between different teams or shifts. For instance, a manufacturer that has three production shifts might have shift 1 follow process set A, shift 2 follow process set B, and shift 3 follow process set C. In doing this, the organization iterates toward the shared vision of the ideal outcome.

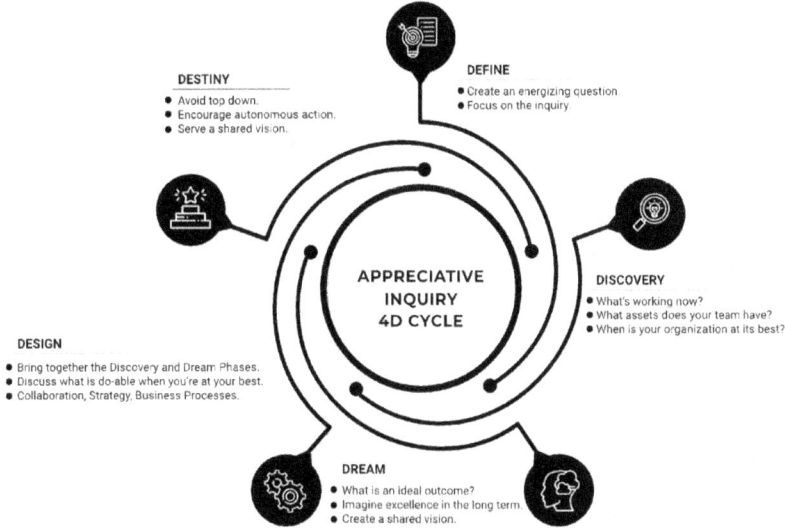

Let's pause for a moment to tie all this together with a hypothetical example. In the description of the define phase, we mentioned the example of quality defects on the factory line. Applying Appreciative Inquiry to this problem may look something like this…

1. **Define:** We have 10% defects on the factory line and our organization's operational standard is less than 5%. We should call a meeting or draft a project proposal focused on: how can we create the best possible product for our customers through optimizing our quality control

processes? (Remember that a critical part of this phase is defining the problem positively to foster excitement, ambition, and creativity).

2. **Discovery:** Next, let's consider what assets and resources we can deploy to improve quality control.

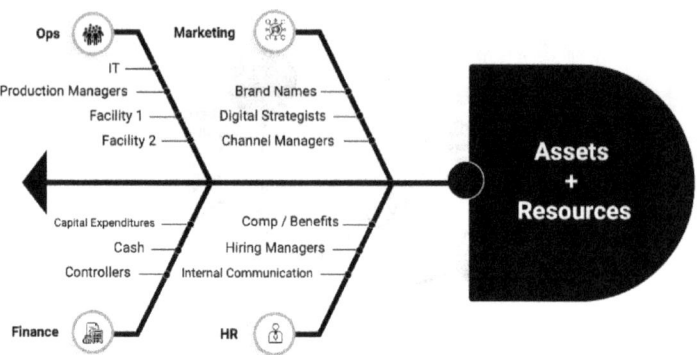

In this example, we might begin by considering key functional areas that influence quality control: communications/human resources, quality management, supervisors, and frontline teams. From these "bones," we can consider more specific assets.

We can adjust compensation and benefits to reward greater attention to quality. We can use flexible staffing models to make sure employees are well rested and can focus. We can increase the ratio of supervisors to employees to reduce errors, or we can invest in quality control training. We can analyze our processes to find those responsible for most quality control errors, or we can invest in technologies that prevent defects. We can redesign the work environment to reduce distractions and invest in technology or training to simplify processes.

3. **Dream:** Once we articulate a long-term, shared vision of ideal quality control outcomes, we may look to leading firms, or even other industries, to see what excellence in quality looks like. Examples of success should be starting points for dreaming even bigger. Of course, we should leverage the creativity and insight of internal resources primarily.

    We might say we want to approach perfection—in five years we'll have less than 1% quality defects. We'll have highly trained, competent supervisors and frontline workers and state-of-the-art production processes and technology to make this happen. In the dream scenario, what new processes would we have? How would staff behave? What technology would serve us? The dreaming process is to set a very assertive target, then imagine what would be necessary to reach that goal.

4. **Design:** The dream step can feel a little ambiguous, or not sufficiently "ground-level." That's where the design phase comes in. We might think of the dream as a horizon 1,000 miles away to move toward. Whereas in the design phase, we outline the next steps to make genuine progress toward that horizon. Here, we also look back at our analysis in the discovery phase to understand how we can align assets and resources to support consistent progress toward the shared vision.

    This phase is thorough and contextualized with the actual circumstances of the organization; below is a simplified example of how this might look.
    - Over the next two months, we'll provide twenty hours of supplemental quality assurance training for relevant supervisory and frontline workers.

- Over the next six months, we will, for relevant employees, include a small bonus tied to year-over-year reduction in the quality defects percentage.
- We'll also offer two extra five-minute breaks throughout the day to reduce employees' cognitive fatigue.
- Over the next year, we'll increase the ratio of quality control supervisors to frontline employees by 10%.
- Quality management and operations leadership will audit the workplace environment to reduce distractions, debris, or other hazards that might contribute to increased quality defects.
- Over the next two years, we'll work with an engineering consultant to design new equipment to automate several of the complex tasks line workers perform.
- Before the end of time horizon, we'll implement a new enterprise resource planning (ERP) cloud with innovative quality control applications.

5. **Destiny:** We'll share this vision with, and welcome feedback from, all levels of the organization. It will empower frontline and supervisors to design and experiment with approaches to improving quality. The destiny phase is cyclical as various levels of the organization iterate toward the ideal outcomes of the shared vision. Perhaps one production manager offers a 5% bonus if quality defects are reduced within the next three months. Perhaps one shift of workers find they reduce quality defects when they take three ten-minute breaks instead of one thirty-minute break. An effective organization will drive progress both top-down and bottom-up.

Could your business benefit from a happiness-promoting, problem-solving model? A model that fosters positivity will ultimately lead to greater success. Appreciative Inquiry begins with an ambition for greater effectiveness and performance.

This model works so well because it's designed with this dynamic in mind. In the discovery and dream phases, people get excited as they identify organizational strengths and uncover opportunities. Excitement continues to build as they think in terms of an ideal vision. This creates an energy and enthusiasm that informs design. And, having empowered employees to take autonomous action, we capture this wave of positive momentum in the destiny phase.

Compare that to the antiquated approach of identifying an issue, running it up the corporate ladder, then implementing a hierarchically imposed singular solution. A positivity-grounded approach blows the doors off the traditional problem-solving model. It will encourage agility, effectiveness, and flourishing within your organization.

As amazing as Appreciative Inquiry is, it's imperfect. You'll still have a variety of personalities sitting at tables looking for solid ideas. Sometimes personalities will clash. Some people will be cynical. And sometimes problems are really friggin' challenging! However, the degree to which you can positively energize the task is predictive of success. Experiment with using this framework. We can easily implement it in simple, everyday meetings and massive, long-term projects.

The learning in the next chapter complements this model. There, we'll look at actively managing the emotional context of your workplace.

APPRECIATIVE INQUIRY

Reflections:

1) How well does your current problem-solving approach work? Does it contribute to or detract from positive culture?
2) What's a key project where you could apply the appreciative inquiry model?
   a. How would you define the problem or outcome?
   b. What assets can you discover to work on the problem or outcome?
   c. What's your aspirational vision (dream)?
   d. What are the incremental steps to get there (design)?
   e. When and how can you make progress (destiny)?

Actions:

1)

2)

3)

Chapter 18

Creating Positive Emotional Context:
Five Best Practices

Have you had a summer job from hell? I had a few during my university years. Looking back on them, I marvel at the variety of weird tasks I was involved in. Perhaps one that was particularly odd was taking part in the demolition of a parking garage.

The job was this: 1) show up at work with steel-toed boots and a hard hat. They provided safety glasses and a flimsy dust mask. 2) Pick up your assigned eighty-pound jackhammer from a storage shed and heft it to the parking garage (at the time, the jackhammer was about half my weight). 3) Receive the assignment of one square yard of the garage floor. 4) Spend the next eight hours standing in the assigned square, jackhammering the ridiculously hard cement to a depth of six inches. 4) After eight hours, return the jack hammer to the shed.

I'm not kidding. This was the entire job. Eight hours of mind-numbing, body-shaking jackhammering while standing in one spot. But wait! It gets better. There were about thirty other underpaid people there too. To have thirty jackhammers going, you needed about ten industrial-sized, trailered-in air compressors. Can you imagine the sound? It must've been over 200 decibels and yes, we wore headphone ear protection, but even with the "earmuffs," the sound was deafening. Within twenty minutes of starting, the space filled with concrete dust. Not a little dust, but a cloud so thick you could barely see the floor. The safety glasses kept the many rock chips from penetrating my eyes, but they did nothing to keep the pervasive quantity of dust out. The paper dust mask would get so coated with silica dust (a known carcinogen) that in order to breathe at all, you'd have to take it off and shake the damn thing out periodically.

Most workers didn't last a day. Seriously! By noon, the thirty people that started the day were down to twenty. My roommate quit by 10 a.m. on the first day. I lasted three days. When I told my boss at the end of the third day that I was *so* done, he warmly shook my numb hand and thanked me profusely. His warm smile and sincere gratitude stand out these many decades later. Although I'm not sure if his warmth was out of gratitude as much as guilt for the early death he was bringing us. Lol.

I expect you don't have working conditions as tough as that. Thank goodness! But could your work environment be materially better? Could warm gratitude *before* I quit have kept me longer? What else could my jackhammer supervisor have done to keep me around? Simply put, could the job have sucked less?

In the last chapter, we established that Appreciative Inquiry is a critical framework to systematically nurture positivity, creativity, and inspiration within your organization. Similarly, there are understated, easy-to-use tools that, when applied consistently, foster positive impact and engagement in the workplace.

1. Facilitate Positivity First

How often is your work filled with conversation about what's going well? Or is your organization like many businesses where most conversations are about problems, what needs fixing, and sources of concern?

The numbers count: something as simple as the ratio of positive to negative interactions is a significant predictor of well-being and performance. For example, research by Marcial Losada showed that a 3:1 ratio of positive to negative interactions among sales teams was highly predictive of profitability.[37] Teams with a 1:1 ratio performed poorly. Teams at a ratio of 2:1, were also poor performers. But once they hit a tipping point of 3:1, teams were more inspired, emotionally invested, optimistic, and showed a major uptick in performance.

Interestingly, this relationship between the positive-negative ratio and performance didn't drop off after the 3:1 tipping point. Returns continued. Teams with even higher ratios, such as 3.5:1 and 4:1, continued to perform even better across metrics such as profitability, customer satisfaction, peer evaluation, etc.

Note that this research has faced criticism in the last few years from some parts of the academic community. That criticism is largely around the specifics of his mathematical calculations and formulas. The overarching lesson that teams with more positive than negative interactions thrive remains well supported.

Something as simple as counting the number of positive versus negative interactions matters for organizational effectiveness.

One of the easiest ways to improve this ratio is as follows. Whenever you start a meeting, even an informal group discussion, begin by asking what's going well.

Having taught this intervention countless times, I can tell you what's likely going to happen when you try this. People will give a superficial, glancing remark about something going well and immediately dive back into focusing on problems. This isn't something to take personally; it's simply a matter of us collectively training the business brain to operate in problem-solving mode.

It may go something like this: "Oh, yeah, we had a good week last week. The assembly line was at 102% expected outcomes. But,

---

[37] Fredrickson & Losada "Positive Affect and the Complex Dynamics of Human Flourishing" published in *American Psychologist*.

CREATING POSITIVE EMOTIONAL CONTEXT: FIVE BEST PRACTICES

you know, we still have this big issue with line number four. I'm worried about the power supply…"

I see this repeatedly. Individuals fail to celebrate, elaborate, and marinate in the positive news. What does this mean for you? Quality leaders will continuously require teams to recognize and reflect on what's going well.

This works on two levels: 1) it leads to the positive emotional reaction that comes from recognizing achievement. Simple. True. It feels good. And 2) an inquisitive leader will say things like, "Well, how did you do that?", "Why did that work?" and "Tell me more." Then, as the person talks more about how they achieved that outcome, it's instructive to others in the room.

In large, mature businesses, singular and impactful change is rare. Rather, it's consistent, incremental improvements, like the ones generated by asking "what's going well," that will drive exceptional outcomes. Every time these discussions occur, other managers have new ideas to apply to their divisions or teams, effectively distributing these incremental improvements throughout the organization.

Starting meetings with the question, "what's going well?" and inviting people to discuss further, is a simple lever for driving continuous improvement. This doesn't have to be formal, either. For example, when you're passing someone in the hall, you might say, "Hey Mike, I really wanted to talk to you about XYZ. But before we get into it, why don't you tell me what's going well with your team right now?"

The other person might laugh it off and think you're being goofy, but if you stick with it, they'll play the game. After a bit, they'll know the drill—start with something positive. Then, almost by default, they'll develop an excitement for meetings or discussions with you because they know they'll have a moment to share what's going well. (Imagine that; positive anticipation for a meeting!)

2. Create Social Catalysts

Another strategy to create positive emotional contexts is to begin meetings with fun and engaging questions. It helps make them personal.

This may sound trivial or even silly, but these small actions to create a positive emotional context are crucial. For example, one research paper found that asking someone what their favorite movie is causes a 27% increase in endorphins (hormones that decrease pain and increase relaxation and joy).[38] The recollection, and anticipation, of positive things makes us happier in the moment. This positive boost is just the beginning.

A second reason this use of social catalysts is so important is that we don't trust and collaborate well with those we don't know. Author Scott Halford suggests that collaboration can only flourish once we get to know people personally.[39] This is true because the release of the brain hormone oxytocin, which is only stimulated in real, personal relationships, builds trust. This is even more pressing when considering the rapid growth in virtual workplaces. The micro-interactions that occurred in the halls, waiting to start meetings, or at the proverbial water cooler are no longer present. So, getting to know coworkers is much less organic.

There's even research to suggest that subconsciously detecting pheromones (released chemical scents that trigger a social response in others) plays a significant role in building trust. Between 70%–93% of communication is nonverbal.[40] And most of these nonverbal communications are absent in virtual work environments. All this is to say that now more than ever, activities that catalyze social

---

[38] 2006, Lee S. Berk of Loma Linda University.
[39] Scott Halford's *Activate Your Brain: How Understanding Your Brain Can Improve Your Work - and Your Life.*
[40] See Dr. Albert Mehrabian's book – *Nonverbal Communication.*

connection are essential for cultivating collaborative, trust-filled, and high-performing environments.

Here's a list of questions that can quickly create an energizing emotional context.

- What's your favorite movie?
- Where's your favorite place you've vacationed?
- Tell me about the best pet you've ever had.
- If you could have dinner with anyone, who would it be?
- What would a perfect day look like for you?
- This list and much more is available for free at www.HappinessMeansBusiness.com/BPP

3. Share Good News

Leaders must make it a point for workers to share good news deliberately. This can be internal or external. Many great ideas come from cross-functional collaboration within the firm. Make it a point to celebrate the entire organization. Perhaps the sales team implemented a new project management framework that increased productivity by 15%. That's great news, and it's something for other divisions to know about.

This applies to external news as well: the labor market has improved, new regulations seem favorable, consumer trends look attractive, etc. You want workers to feel an increased sense of optimism about the business's potential. And that's not to be dishonest or manipulative; it's simply setting up a context that's accurate and positive. Leaders tend to do the opposite with news. They focus on threats (remember the negativity bias from earlier). Daily news media constantly bombard us with messages of negativity already. You want to counterbalance this natural bias toward the negative by deliberately sharing the positive.

The best way for this kind of sharing to work is in conversation. "News" can be a standing agenda item at regular meetings. It can be something leaders intentionally share in conversation. And, of course, it can come in more staid communication mediums like newsletters, emails, and intranet notices.

4. Admit Mistakes

This idea may seem like a different flavor, but it's another critical component of a positive emotional context. Perhaps the present political American situation is the best example of how dysfunctional people can be with bad news or mistakes. You may recall the news of the Taliban rout of the Afghan government following the withdrawal of U.S. troops in the summer of 2021. This was obviously an unplanned, unexpected, and overwhelming failure. It's likely that the Pentagon had ways they could've managed the exit more effectively and mitigated much of the harm to soldiers, allies, and civilians. Regardless of partisan preference, it's easy to see things could've been handled better.

But the thing is, almost nowhere in political circles has there been any admission that they handled the withdrawal poorly. No one has stepped up to take ownership of what didn't go well. That's because, in the political arena, to admit fault or weakness is blood in the water for sharks waiting to strike. One would hope that you aspire to have your organization function more gracefully than the current political scene (which isn't a high bar at all).

To make it so, remember that there is a degree of trust in smaller organizations or teams within larger organizations. There's also an intimacy of knowledge, as people know where mistakes were made. In such settings, the ability of leaders and team members to say, "you know, I could've done that better," or "I regret that things turned out this way," makes all the difference. In addition, research has found it triggers an empathy response in the listener toward the speaker. Listeners are far more receptive to the mistake itself and the person who made it. This paves the way for honest discussions instead of gossip, discord, and dysfunction.

So, perhaps counterintuitively, you should make admitting wrongs the norm. Doing this will promote a culture where you and your people are closer. And you'll have productive, honest discussions about how to move forward.

5. Use a Formal Strengths Assessment

I highly recommend using a formal strengths assessment for members of your team. An easy, affordable (about $20 per test) place to start is the Gallup Strengths Finder Assessment 2.0. This assessment tool is exceptionally well-validated by scientific literature. Further, it's more reliable than most of the common Meyers-Briggs-inspired approaches which ask users to evaluate themselves in terms of dichotomies (e.g., introverted or extroverted). Most functional adults fall toward the middle of the spectrum on these things and include, for instance, both introverted and extroverted tendencies. So, these black-and-white outputs, "I'm an ENTJ," are usually less helpful oversimplifications.

The Strengths Finder assessment gives the user a list of their top five strengths from among a list of thirty-four options. Of course, these results are useful for the user. It helps people give language to the things they're naturally good at and boosts self-esteem. But where this assessment excels is in its ability to help third parties (such as leaders and managers) be more objective in understanding what contributions individuals can make. For instance, if I, as a leader, have a meeting coming up for a sensitive, cross-functional initiative, I can select someone from my team to lead the meeting who I know has strong characteristics like empathy, collaboration, and interpersonal relations.

Beyond this specific case, the Strengths Finder also empowers leaders to assign team members tasks that are most aligned with their strengths. This isn't only a nice-to-have, but a major boost to employee engagement and productivity.

A final note here is the importance of considering strengths in the hiring process. The default approach to hiring goes something like this: a manager, or senior leader, thinks, "I'm good at this job. That's why I've been put in charge after all. More people like me would be helpful to have on the team." And they end up hiring someone like themself. This isn't a criticism of hiring managers; it's just often the unintentional thought process driven by subconscious beliefs and biases.

Instead, leaders should hire to fill gaps in the strengths profile of their team. So, they look at their own strengths and the strengths of their team members and say, "based on our deficiencies, we need someone high on strategy, ideas, achievement, etc." This is one of the most underrated ways to upskill a management team.

Consider your own team. Do you have many people with similar strengths? Do you have gaps your next hire could fill?

In this chapter, we covered five best practices you can implement right now to nurture positive emotional contexts in your organization. In your meetings, lead with positivity first, encourage social catalysts, and share good news. Set a precedent for individuals to admit their mistakes and recognize and share their strengths freely.

Next, let's consider the impact of emotional intelligence.

CREATING POSITIVE EMOTIONAL CONTEXT: FIVE BEST PRACTICES

Reflection:

1) What do you think the typical positive-negative ratio is for interactions within your organization? How might this be improved?
2) What's your favorite movie, and why did you make that choice? How do you feel as you think about it?
3) What's some good news for your company (internal or external)?
4) When was the last time you witnessed someone step up to take ownership of their mistake? How do you feel about it?
5) What do you think are your top five strengths? Do they correspond to what you found in the Gallup Strengths Finder? (See actions below.)

Actions:

1) Access resources at the link provided to use at the start of your next meeting.
2) Complete and share your results from the Gallup Strengths Finder 2.0 and encourage your team members to do so as well.
3)

Chapter 19

Emotional Intelligence

A friend of mine, Hernandez, is smart, genuinely caring, and thoughtful. On a recent occasion, he told me his next-door neighbor was blowing his lawn clear of fallen leaves. My friend was annoyed. The darn blower made a racket and disturbed his late afternoon relaxation. That evening, Hernandez went out to walk his dog, and noticed a few leaves that were on his neighbor's lawn were now on his lawn. My friend, playing his old, well-worn default pattern, saw himself as a *victim*!

The offending neighbor was out in his driveway and my "*wronged*" friend marched over to confront him… about the… yes… few dozen scattered leaves. With zero self-awareness, Hernandez started a verbal altercation. It didn't go well, ending with ultimatums and threats.

Now, Hernandez's next-door neighbor will hate my friend… passionately… forever!

Oh, my! If I could inject Hernandez with an Emotional Intelligence serum, his life would be infinitely better! But unfortunately, my friend couldn't see his own rising anger and frustration or read the emotional cues his neighbor signaled, and he couldn't regulate his reactions. Because of these inabilities, a minor situation became a serious and irredeemable problem.

Oxford dictionary defines Emotional Intelligence as "the capacity to be aware of, control, and express one's emotions, and to handle interpersonal relationships judiciously and empathetically." Many have studied it extensively.

EMOTIONAL INTELLIGENCE

Contrary to popular belief, emotional intelligence (EQ) isn't a question of nature versus nurture: it's nature *and* nurture. It's both genetic (present at birth) and acquired (through environmental factors and/or learning).

We can observe natural differences in disposition in the earliest periods of life. For instance, female babies spend more time gazing at the faces of their caregivers than male babies do. While girls are doing this, they're learning nuanced facial expressions. These tendencies continue throughout childhood. Consider the typical four-year-old boy. Often, he's likely to engage in an activity-oriented style of play. This may look like joining with other boys to play with toy trucks. They'll make sounds, drive their trucks around, and crash into things. The activity of playing with toys is the focal point. This is referred to as parallel play—together but focused on activity. A four-year-old girl is more likely to spend time in social-oriented play: she's likely to join other girls in conversations and interactions facilitated by their toys. The engagement with other girls is the focal point.

Again, it's important to note that these examples don't hold true for *all* boys and girls, but there are well-researched patterns. What's more, these patterns in childhood are highly predictive of emotional intelligence levels later in life. Overall, women have higher levels of emotional intelligence than men do. This is a nuanced difference. Men typically score higher than women in certain areas of emotional intelligence, such as self-regulation.

Another interesting observation from the science of emotional intelligence is that EQ is highly correlated with IQ. That's not to say one causes the other or that all intelligent people are emotionally intelligent. But the two tend to show up together.

So, it's no surprise that those who rise to the ranks of senior leadership in an organization typically (not always) have a high degree of emotional intelligence. Consider how they had both great strategy (intelligence) and worked networking opportunities to build important relationships (emotional intelligence). Most senior leaders spend their entire careers getting ahead through emotional intelligence.

What's more, individuals with high IQ who want to develop EQ are far more receptive to training than their lower IQ counterparts. And as you'll see, this sort of training is essential.

Harvard Business Review Analytics Services did a comprehensive study[41] on teaching emotional intelligence and found that a high EQ in an organization predicts high employee engagement and customer loyalty, which leads to greater productivity and profitability. Firms that invest in EQ training outperform those that don't. Often, training facilitates greater use of intelligence that was previously unconscious. People already strong in emotional intelligence become exceptionally skilled in its use.

Having outlined the role of nature and nurture in emotional intelligence and its importance for organizational outcomes, here's a closer look at the components of EQ.

1) Self-awareness: Your ability to know how you feel in a moment and understand what your emotions are telling you.
2) Self-regulation: Your capacity to respond in a rational, reasoned way, regardless of how you feel emotionally — how you manage your emotions.
3) Motivation: Your willingness to take initiative and work toward an outcome.
4) Empathy: Your ability to feel what others are feeling. Note that this doesn't mean just recognizing it but internalizing that recognition — feeling with them.

---

[41] The EI Advantage: Driving Innovation and Business Success through the Power of Emotional Intelligence, Harvard Business Review, August 12, 2019.

5) Social skills: This covers your broader set of tendencies; your ability to get along with others, communicate effectively, etc.

Taken together, these components of EQ are often referred to in business simply as "people skills." Success as a leader has an obvious and profound connection to how well we connect with others. That connection is a two-way street. It's not just that the leader perceives they get along well with others. More importantly, it's how others feel when they're around that leader.

When you have all these "people skills" you're considered highly emotionally intelligent.

What if you don't?

As mentioned at the outset, there's an acquired component for EQ. It can be learned.

A key point for this training is that it should *not* revolve around personality assessments or in-depth analysis of people's current EQ skills. That's because those approaches focus people's attention on specific areas identified as deficiencies. This can lead to insecurity, resistance, and bias toward the negative.

The most practical training approach is grounded in mindfulness. This is perhaps the first EQ intervention workplaces should invest in. It's basic training. That's because mindfulness is the awareness of one's current state; it's being conscious of the here and now. There are many ways to practice mindfulness: meditation, yoga, deep breathing, and even bilateral exercises like running or swimming can produce a meditative state in some individuals (lucky them). With mindfulness, not only is the ability to recognize emotional states increased, but so is the ability to self-regulate one's responses.

Innovative leaders are investing in mindfulness training in their workplaces. They also create suitable physical spaces for meditation.

A second tenet of effective EQ training is the practice of sharing feelings. This simply means we create cultures where feelings are validated, accepted, and have a range beyond the male caricatures of leadership limited to angry dissatisfaction and cheerful backslapping.

A simple exercise to improve emotional recognition is playing short videos or animated images and asking observers to identify what the person is feeling. We can train people specifically by showing them images of the seven universal emotions.[42] Emotions like sadness, happiness, and fear are universally recognizable. But depending on the degree of the expression, some people can't recognize the emotions on others' faces. Again, on average, men have more difficulty with such recognition.

There are more subtle training protocols as well. Often when I'm teaching EQ, I'll set it up as role-playing within a work situation. This is effective because it makes trainees feel like they're being trained on a work-related skill rather than a personal deficiency. For example, I might set up a customer service role-play and work with employees on empathizing with the customer, paraphrasing what the customer responded, and self-regulating emotions before responding. This effectively trains the key skills of EQ while still feeling work-related.

A third strategy for increasing EQ is encouraging leaders to join in the trenches. This is empathy exemplified!

Leaders often feel they have to be great at something to jump in and lead by example, or that they're too important for "grunt work." Neither is true. By not joining in the fray of the frontline work, they may be perceived as thinking themselves too important to do the "dirty work." Doing the work of others—even doing it badly—has the opposite effect expected. As a leader, it shows tremendous humility and vulnerability to jump into an unfamiliar or challenging situation to help your team when they're struggling. Here's a powerful example that I was fortunate enough to see firsthand.

---

[42] The exact number of so-called universal emotions is up for debate, but scholars agree that several emotional expressions are physically expressed the same way in every society.

Remember the prison I mentioned before? Of the many ugly situations that arise in a jail, one of the worst things employees had to deal with was when mentally ill prisoners threw tantrums, including throwing their own excrement around the jail cell. Prison overcrowding meant there'd often be another inmate in the cell cowering in a corner as the display unfolded. Under these circumstances the prison employees must do what's called an extraction: an emergency intervention where guards enter with protective equipment (shields and clubs) to remove the volatile prisoner and take him to the clinic or solitary confinement.

After I implemented positive EQ interventions at this prison, I learned about one of these extractions: specifically, I heard about it because something happened that had never happened before. A debriefing always follows an extraction where they report injuries, execution, what went well, and what could be improved. As on every occasion, everyone knew what to expect at the end of the debriefing: the most junior person would be told to clean the cell — a most unpleasant job! Instead, the assistant deputy warden, the most senior person on the extraction team, said, "I can't ask any of you to do something I wouldn't do myself." He announced he'd be the one to clean the cell. So, he donned the full-body biohazard suit and did it himself.

Can you imagine how this rippled through this organization? Within twenty-four hours, everybody heard about it. It was symbolic of the change taking place. Employees heard these cultural changes were underway, but now they really believed it!

Mindfulness, working with feelings, and leading by example are three critical elements of building emotional intelligence within an organization. Leaders should focus on fostering a culture and business systems that value emotional intelligence. High-performing firms will teach EQ, role-model EQ, and hire for EQ.

Next, let's compare and contrast select leadership styles.

Reflection:

1) What are the components of emotional intelligence?
2) What is the emotional intelligence level of leadership in your organization?
3) Can you think of a time when you, or someone you know, failed to recognize the emotions of others?
4) What's something you enjoy doing that could be a mindfulness-building practice?
5) Can you think of a time when a manager or senior leader joined you in the trenches? How did it feel?

Actions:

1) Brainstorm mindfulness training, emotional recognition, and/or role-modeling exercises to try.

2) Identify the core values that would shape expectations in your organization's code of conduct.

3)

Chapter 20

Whole-Brain Leadership

Imagine reporting to someone who thinks they're "the boss" because they're inherently superior to other people — all other people. Consider autocratic leaders: take Kim Jong-un, the head of state in North Korea. The mythology around his place in society is that God appointed him (and his father before him) to lead their nation. Perhaps with less divine silliness, other autocratic leaders similarly have absolute rule over every aspect of their business or country. This isn't a new thing.

"Divine" leaders are as old as human civilization!

Absent other models, corporate structures evolved over the last several hundred years, primarily from ancient military structures. War, and the organizational structures to carry out war, have been around for thousands of years. Until relatively recently, monarch-led nations were led by people literally seen as appointed by God. He, and on rare occasions, she, had an ultimate, divine status that kept them separate from those fighting the wars.

The frontline soldiers were peons. They were devoid of dignity and unworthy of respect by the king and his senior leaders. Soldiers were capital, much like spears and wagons, as opposed to human beings. These structures were extremely hierarchical, with much separation between top and bottom, and they organized military units by rank. The monarch gave orders to a handful of generals, who then gave orders to their subordinates, who had subordinates, and so on. This is the model from which corporate structures were born.

(Note there are historical exceptions to this rule, as one of our clients who happened to be an amateur military historian kindly pointed out to us during a training session, but on the whole this was the norm…)

These early military structures were completely male dominated. They had a narrow focus: defeat the enemy. This focus led to rational, assertive, and often aggressive leadership styles still associated with power today.

We know this doesn't feel great. And there are still inklings of this in nearly all of today's organizations. That being said, we're in an era of "democratizing" our workplaces. It's unclear what exactly this looks like. But it's a deep desire that work become more than just taking orders for a paycheck. We want a working life that satisfies the soul in a way that we previously hadn't expected from our employers.

At the time of this writing, there's an incredibly tight labor market, resulting in record-low unemployment numbers and a massive churn in the workforce. The popular press is calling this period "The Great Resignation." Droves of workers are leaving their organizations for something better. What's better? It's rarely articulated this succinctly, but put simply, people want to be happier at work.

This chapter will explain the nuances of whole-brain leadership skills and what I call "feminine leadership," as well as why these concepts are critical to success in the future of business. I'll elaborate on this below, but "feminine" here refers to attributes and traits that all of us have but tend to be more embodied in female psychology.

Whole-brain leaders have a strong balance of analytical and intuitive skills. According to Accenture, they blend "what's traditionally been considered 'left-brain' (scientific) skills that draw on data analysis and critical reasoning with 'right-brain' (creative) skills that draw on areas like intuition and empathy."[43]

---

[43] Geoff Hudson-Searle, executive director and best-selling author, "Emotional Intelligence and Your Survival through the 4th Industrial Revolution!" on LinkedIn.

We'll go beyond this definition of whole-brain leadership to discuss the masculine and feminine attributes of thinking and leading and consider how they might be better balanced.

In popular culture, we hold military figures as exemplars of strong leadership skills. Of course, there are military leaders who shine as models of holistic leadership, but the common image of a take-charge, no-nonsense, tough-as-nails, and *always male* leadership dynamic is absurd. It excludes half the population and most of our collective character traits as sources of good leadership.

Leaders too often express power as militant and overwhelmingly macho. I call this leadership style "command and control." It's the default model in organizations. It's what we're socially conditioned to accept, and it is continuously role modeled.

In brief, time-bound emergency situations, we all want "command and control" styles of management. When the proverbial fire is burning, and the house is at risk of falling, we want strong, confident direction. We want a clear chain of command that takes charge. But, outside of these rare instances, it usually is counterproductive, undermines collaboration and breeds resentment.

Today's leaders can and must do much better. There are three compelling reasons business must modernize the default leadership style: 1) profound changes in the new economy compel organizations to reform their leadership practices; 2) to take advantage of skill sets that stereotypically aren't harnessed when pursuing effective leadership; and 3) there's an ethical imperative, considering the historically patriarchal origins of corporate structures.

The new economy requires new leadership. Speed of change, complex relationships, diverse shareholder interests, increased government regulations, and complete globalization characterize the so-called Fourth Industrial Revolution. What's more, in large, diversified corporations, there are tremendous varieties of products and services that need to fall under a shared vision for the organization.

To highlight the speed and profound disruption in our economy, consider that someone could design something on their iPhone this afternoon, 3D prints it in China tomorrow, and have it available for sale on multiple online platforms in less than forty-eight hours. A 2015 study by the World Economic Forum observed that there's a common belief that because the world is becoming so technologically advanced, the skill sets of tomorrow will be technical (STEM—science, technology, engineering, and math). But these technical skills are being turned into commodities. Think about the sweeping IT outsourcing to places like India and Bangladesh.

The real leadership skill sets necessary are the capacity to manage the ongoing torrent of economic, technological, and cultural change in the modern business environment.

The top ten most sought-after skills, according to the World Economic Forum study mentioned above, are:

(1) complex problem solving
(2) critical thinking
(3) creativity
(4) people management
(5) coordinating with others
(6) emotional intelligence
(7) judgment and decision making
(8) service orientation
(9) negotiation
(10) cognitive flexibility

Arguably, many of these skills are more readily found in women,[44] given how most of them rely on the sixth foundational

---

[44] Meshat and Nejati "Does Emotional Intelligence Depend on Gender?" published in Sage Open 2017.

item: high levels of emotional intelligence. Now, please keep in mind that we're speaking in terms of averages here. There are quite a few exceptions to these on-average gender differences. For instance, not all women excel in emotional intelligence and not all men are deficient. But overall, women are stronger in this area.

This isn't a criticism of men or mere posturing for political correctness, it's a reality supported by neuroscience and social psychology. Biologically, women have greater right-brain-oriented thinking processes. The right-brain orientation includes things like creativity, intuition, and emotionality. Conversely, men have a greater left-brain orientation, making their thinking more compartmentalized, logic-driven, and analytical.

I don't want to overemphasize the differences between men and women. But I want to clarify that what I call "feminine leadership skills" are essential to an organization's success.

One of the key skills of feminine leadership is multifactorial thinking — the ability to think about multiple things at once (the opposite of compartmentalized thinking). When we observe how a male leader typically runs a meeting, it includes a linear agenda: "First, we'll talk about budget, then customer satisfaction, then regulatory concerns." The meeting unfolds in chunks focused on each topic.

When women run meetings, they usually hold the key topics in a shared awareness: "Let's talk about budget, customer satisfaction, and regulatory concerns." Those topics aren't seen as separate. The capacity to hold and engage simultaneously with multiple streams of thought is critical to success in today's business environment.

"People management" and "coordinating with others" (skills 4 and 5) also depend on capacity for emotional intelligence. EQ also influences judgment and decision making (skill 7).

Women are more balanced with judgment and decision-making. Quality research shows firms with a high representation of female senior leaders have fewer ethical lapses.[45] This is grounded in biological differences between genders. Men are driven by testosterone which promotes assertiveness and risk-taking, which is great, and a necessary part of a healthy organization. But when it's out of balance, it leads to excessive risk, recklessness, and even unethical behavior.

Other studies suggest that a preponderance of female leadership is associated with better financial performance, more effective communication, and greater innovation. So, there's ample evidence that this drawing out and harnessing of leadership skill sets that are more commonly found in women is critical for success in the new economy.

There's a lingering bias toward masculine leadership given the military history of corporations outlined in this chapter and other longstanding cultural norms. Therefore, in pursuing whole-brain leadership, you must advocate for an increased emphasis on feminine leadership qualities. In doing so, you'll create a more balanced organizational leadership model that fully embraces left-brain, masculine attributes, and right-brain, feminine attributes of leadership.

Your organization should advocate, train, and hire for these feminine leadership skill sets. This doesn't mean hiring or favoring women over men, although you may have diversity and inclusion reasons to encourage this. Instead, your major motivation must be to promote these skill sets within the organization. Because, as suggested in this chapter, the success of tomorrow's organizations is determined by their willingness to recognize and nurture whole-brain leadership.

---

[45] Offerman and Foley offer a comprehensive review of the research in this meta-analysis: *"Is there a Female Leadership Advantage?"* published in the Oxford Research Encyclopedia, Business and Management - February 28, 2020.

If your organization had a healthy infusion of feminine leadership traits, how would that influence the retention of your key staff? Faced with workforces demanding a "democratization" of workplace mechanisms, what difference could your business make with a balancing of whole-brained leadership?

In the next chapter, we'll roll up our sleeves and do the work most of us hate to do. We tackle attitude problems and poison personalities!

Reflections:

1) In your professional experience, have you observed differences in left vs. right- brained or masculine vs. feminine leadership attributes?
2) What are the key skills for future business leaders? Which ones fall more toward masculine leadership? Which ones fall more toward feminine leadership?
3) What is multifactorial thinking as opposed to compartmentalized thinking?
4) How can you nurture feminine and whole-brain leadership within your organization?

WHOLE-BRAIN LEADERSHIP

Actions:

1)

2)

3)

Chapter 21

Running Toward Attitude Problems

In 2018, a client of mine, Cheryl Stefani, asked me to give a talk about positive psychology to her department's staff. She stated she wanted my message to be upbeat and encouraging. As always, I inquired about the specifics of the emotional tone of her team.

She said she had a happy, hardworking staff, and they wanted the boost of positivity my teaching would provide. I was curious. If they're so happy, why did they need the boost of positivity?

Cheryl said, "Well, despite the great work we do, and the great attitude and teamwork, sometimes it's hard to come to work and be in a good mood."

"Why is that?" I asked.

Cheryl admitted, "To be honest, we have one difficult staff member. She's extremely negative about everything. She complains about our customers, the organization, and her personal life. Nothing is good enough for her. It would be okay if she kept all her opinions to herself, but she doesn't. She's loud about her many judgments. I know she brings the team down sometimes."

I'd seen this scenario many times before. I gave her the talk she wanted, but I taught with an emphasis on team dynamics. I explained how emotions are like the weather. An individual's storm rains on everybody. I coached Cheryl. I said that following my talk, she'd have the perfect opportunity to speak with her negative team member. With the awareness I'd bring to the office about how negative people impact everyone around them, Cheryl would have an opening. Her staff member would hear my teaching and never suspect that any part of it was deliberately directed at her. Yet she'd see herself in my warnings.

Cheryl followed up and confronted her problem employee. She had several tough conversations. A few months later, I was at her office on other business, and we ran into each other. Cheryl excitedly said, "You wouldn't believe the amount of change I've seen since you gave your talk!"

"Really?" I asked. "What's different"?

Cheryl then regaled me on how she had challenging conversations with her individual, problematic staff member. There were tears! There were defensive denials! There was the involvement of a shop steward and accusations that Cheryl was harassing this unfortunate employee. Then there was a dramatic admission—the problem employee said she loves her job. Her role at the office is one of the few areas of her life that's "in control" and fulfilling. She committed to support the people she worked with. To Cheryl's surprise, the employee even said she loved some of her colleagues. Their presence in her life was important to her, and she never wanted to hurt any of them.

That was the beginning of a radical, positive change.

Earlier in the book, we touched on the idea of "emotional contagion." On a subconscious level, we constantly read and feel the emotions of others. This pattern is particularly pronounced with leaders and influencers in an organization. When leaders display positive or negative emotions, they are immediately picked up and felt by those around them. This emotional contagion happens in less than 33 milliseconds (that's an astonishing 33 thousandths of a second).

Surely, you've seen the dangers of emotional contagion. You've seen how one person can ruin the entire mood of a group or workplace. These can be people who resent their employers, feel contempt for customers, or have otherwise troubled lives that bleed into the workplace. Individuals like this are <u>poison</u> to the organization.

You undoubtedly know people who spread this poison; they're oppositional and divisive, sarcastic and cynical, negative and pessimistic. This attitude — emotional disposition — if apparent for more than a single "bad day," represents a pattern. Rarely will it readily change on its own. These personalities can, and often do, ruin team dynamics. We *must* manage them!

Fortunately, attitudes can be managed. They're not "bad people." After all, we all have some imperfections in our personalities. *It's about behavior*: what they say, their expressions, interactions, and receptivity to learning.

You don't want to overlook that employees are people first with individual worth. Everyone goes through periodic rough patches in their lives, and those hard times often impact work performance and/or attitude. That's why good employers have Employee & Family Assistance Programs (EFAP) that provide outside help. In addition, empathetic leaders help people cope. That said, consistently negative people have no right to take it out on their organization and colleagues regardless of what's driving their disposition.

It's important to remember that humans are emotional, sensitive creatures first, and cognitive, rational thinkers second. So, the notion that your other employees are immune to the effects of certain people's negative emotions is false.

It may seem unnecessary, or even counterproductive, to intervene with employees who have a bad attitude but otherwise perform well. I disagree: these individuals need to be managed as if their attitude problem were a performance problem. Given the emotional contagion, their negative impact on the culture of the organization will far exceed the positive impact of their good work.

I once heard a seminar speaker, a former police officer, ask, "What makes a good cop?" He then answered his question: "Great cops run toward bullets not away from them!"

Great leaders run toward attitude problems not away from them!

RUNNING TOWARD ATTITUDE PROBLEMS

Managers, especially frontline managers, will find that confronting attitude issues is some of the hardest work they do. For that reason, many line managers, supervisors, and even senior managers never take on that work. They often know a specific individual is struggling; *and* that the individual should be let go, or put through coaching, and/or therapy. But it's difficult and intimidating to have these challenging conversations, especially about something as intangible as attitude. So, they avoid it. Left unattended, these problems are cancerous and can undermine the organization.

Some years ago, I worked for a big insurance company. I was the director of a region with three offices and over 200 employees. I handled the annual formal performance review process with my direct-report staff. Nowhere in the prescribed format was there a place where we reviewed attitude. So, recognizing the lack, before getting into the rote part of the performance review, I'd always begin by asking employees to assess their attitude:

"Everybody in an organization either contributes to or takes away from the energy of the workplace. What would you say you do? Do you bring energy or take it away?"

Something interesting happened when I asked this question: a surprising number of people honestly responded they were probably taking away energy. And when the employee says this, it's an open invitation to have a conversation around attitude. Now, if someone said they weren't sure, or that they were probably positive and I felt I knew otherwise, I'd gently push back. I'd point to someone who contributed an exceptional amount of energy and challenge them to reflect on that.

"Well, I'm not sure. Think about Laurie. She's so positive and such a willing helper. She makes a huge contribution to office morale. Do you think you're on the same level? Frankly, I don't see you quite that way…"

This is sensitive territory and requires a delicate balance of forwardness and tact. But if the conversation goes well, it will drive immediate improvement. When compassionate and still honest, attitude management is just like other performance management discussions—we make the other person aware, and they're assisted in adjusting their *behaviors* accordingly.

Of course, some people aren't willing to receive this feedback. They may be resistant or even defiant. If this is true, the manager can't give in. They must manage the attitude issue like it was any other performance issue. That means first coaching toward improvement. And if improvements don't come to bear, then it becomes a labor relations issue which may include discipline or firing.

I once had an employee with a horrible attitude. She was toxic to colleagues. Everyone who had to work with her became discouraged, stressed, and often burnt out. The trouble was that she could reasonably do many aspects of her job and firing or disciplining her was an absolute last resort because of the labor relations policies in place in the unionized environment.

I spent many months working with her attitude issues. It got to where, feeling the pressure from me to change, she got a psychologist to document formal accommodations were necessary for her mental health diagnosis. She'd be entitled to special assignments. This became a golden opportunity to rescue others in the organization from her negativity. In her accommodation requirements, it was noted that she didn't manage interpersonal relationships well, struggled with high volume, and so on and so forth. I seized the opportunity to take all her duties that required interactions with other people away: customers, clients, and colleagues. That effectively restricted her role to a handful of analytical functions within our system.

Our office was a cubicle farm (an open office layout). Everyone had a cubicle except for a few managers. To accommodate her restrictions, I literally built a floor-to-ceiling office for her and set her thirty feet from the nearest worker. The balancing act was to stay committed to her interests *and* protect the energy of the workplace.

It was my responsibility to do everything I could to protect the emotional health and morale of our employees. That's the point of this chapter; that's why I call it *running* toward performance problems. Managers maintain psychological safety and positive emotional contexts for the workforce. *Skirting this responsibility is failed leadership.*

If providing awareness, coaching, and isolating the damage to others is inadequate, then parting with the employee (respectfully and per all legal requirements) is necessary.

This is difficult work—perhaps the most difficult part of leadership. But it's essential. If you manage the negativity that often comes from a few individuals, the difference it makes is huge. At the beginning of the book, I noted the science showing our need for a minimum of a 3:1 ratio of positive to negative interactions. By eliminating chronic negative behaviors, you massively change that ratio. Success follows! Creativity and collaboration abound. It's the lifting of an oppressive weight. It's freedom for your teams to be their best!

Next, we'll look at "coaching" as a way of supervising. It's more than a mindset shift.

Reflections:

1) Even though it happens subconsciously, upon reflection, can you identify times when negative emotions spread from one person to another? What was the impact?
2) Are there any employees in your organization in need of attitude management? How can you address this?
3) How can you bring discussions about attitude into your performance evaluation processes?

Actions:

1)

2)

3)

Chapter 22

Invest in Coaching

Friend: Hey Paul, I know you've been speaking in front of audiences and conducting training for over twenty-five years, but I think you could do a lot better.

Me: Uh-huh.

Friend: Yeah, first off, you start your talk by asking the attendees a few questions. They don't even know you yet. You need to tell a few stories first. You know, get them warmed up to you.

Me: Okay.

Friend: You also need to jazz up your PowerPoint slides with flashy color pictures. People want vivid images that capture their attention. Your slides are boring. Gosh, you even have some slides with just one word on it.

Me: That's true.

Friend: And dude, you must stay on the stage. You always seem to want to get down and walk around. How are the people in the back of the room even going to see you? I'd be happy to give you more advice on this stuff because I really want to support your success.

Me: You're a true friend. Thanks. Let me check my calendar. I'm pretty busy these days.

This is a paraphrased true story. In fact, over the years I've done this work, I can't count the number of times I've received unsolicited offers of advice. Usually, my "advisers" are people who don't make a living training and teaching. They're always well-intended. And, occasionally, I get truly great feedback. Most often, however, I entirely ignore their commentary.

I inherently distrust advice from people who aren't genuine experts. But more than that, I have an ego-based resistance to unsolicited advice. Perhaps I should be much more open-minded and completely enjoy being told how to do my job. But really!

Can you relate? How do you feel when someone, possibly your boss, strolls into your office and offers unsolicited advice? When that boss begins a monologue, maybe even one you've heard more than a few times before, do you sometimes wish they'd just go away? Isn't it especially annoying when they really don't want to hear your perspective on why you approach the work the way you do?

The boss (or friend) thinks they're being helpful. Doesn't everyone who is "training" think they are being helpful? Yet, I think a lot of "training" is a colossal waste. This isn't necessarily because of the content, but it's often a function of format and style.

Anyone with a few years of management experience in a big organization has seen a failed training initiative (or three or four). They make huge investments to develop curriculum, train trainers, and coordinate a massive project to educate hundreds of team members. Operations suffer a major setback when staff aren't doing their job because they're in the classroom. Once they're "trained," they return to the backlog of work and either don't implement the new process or struggle for months learning some new system. Unfortunately, this is common, and it gets even worse when you train for so-called "soft skills" where accountability is difficult to assess.

There's a consensus in organizational psychology that coaching far exceeds training to drive improvements. Traditional training, in a nutshell, comprises telling people what to do. It's not very effective. According to the NTL Institute for Applied Behavioral Science, the average person retains only about 5% of what they hear during a lecture. Further, traditional classroom-style training has a maximum retention of 30% (often less), whereas coaching over several weeks with one-on-one accountability has a retention approaching 80%.[46]

The difference between training and coaching isn't always readily recognizable. Some people think of coaching as what you do with little kids learning to play basketball. They think of it as directed, step-by-step teaching, with a lot of repetition and demonstration. That stereotypical sports-inspired image of coaching isn't what we're getting at. In fact, even in sports, this isn't how coaching looks at the highest level.

Everybody has periods when they aren't at their best. Consider basketball superstar Steph Curry when he had a scoring slump. Would his coach intervene by saying, "hey, I'm going to show you how to shoot a jump shot"? You wouldn't be so silly to offer that advice, even when Steph is in a drought. To alter his mechanics or style would hinder one of the greatest three-point shooters in basketball's history. Instead, what you'd want to do is to be an active problem-solver with Steph.

You might ask him what he did in previous slumps to turn things around. You want him to do the brainstorming. Perhaps he'll uncover that his best spot to shoot from is just outside the three-point line at an 80-degree angle from the rim. So, you'd focus on setting up that shot for him in practice that week.

If that doesn't work, you'd continue with the same line of inquiry as before: "well, last time you had a scoring slump, what worked for you?" Through this process, you're listening for the person being coached (coachee for short) to evaluate their own processes. To coach effectively, you ought to hold the person you're working

---

[46] See selected publications at NTL.org.

with as the wisest person in their own performance. You'd hold Steph accountable to discover his own process and insights for improving.

Steph might say, "I remember in my rookie year, I had several games where I was nervous. I'd miss and be even more nervous the next time down court. I'd look for the pass. My teammates got on me, because even when I was in the clear, I was looking for an outlet. The team chatted about it at halftime one game, and the direction was for me just to shoot. Anytime I had any opportunity, I was told to take the shot. And I did. It started badly, but then the shots fell."

"Perfect," you'd say. "In tonight's game, I want you to shoot a lot. From anywhere you have a step on the defender. We're going to get the ball in your hands, Steph. Just shoot!"

The great coach gives Steph the okay to implement his best plan for himself.

This applies to high-level coaching in all settings. Of course, in business, the extent to which you can hold the individual to be the wisest person in their performance depends on their skills and expertise in relevant areas. On day one of a new job, somebody may not be given as much space or ownership of the coaching process. But you still want to limit how much you tell them what to do. It should be more collaborative and conversational.

As the coach introduces new types of work, they should ask open-ended questions: "What's your experience with this type of thing?" And the coachee will answer. Then the coach (leader) can say, "Great, we do a lot of that the same way, but we do some of it like this… Do you want to try it? How was that? What ideas do you have about how that might be done better? Which of these approaches is most suited to your work style?"

This open-ended question approach gets the coachee to investigate their cognitive processes to understand what works for them. And when they can identify what works for them, they become invested in the solution. That's the ticket to effective coaching. When you lead people through a process of self-discovery, they feel *more invested and motivated* to act than if they're simply told what or how to do things.

As you progress from coaching novices to seasoned professionals, the role of a coach as a thinking partner (as opposed to a lecturer) becomes even more important. For example, let's say you're the operations manager for a large department and one person in your division is a financial analyst with an accounting background. Frankly, unless you're an accountant, you're not well suited to tell them to change how they do Profit and Loss Statements or suggest a better way to structure balance sheets. Instead, you might say, "Hey I've got all this data and I'm trying to convince the board of xyz. Do you have some ideas for how to best do that? How would you approach this? What are the best methods of analysis?"

Again, effective coaching is asking people for their guidance on how they should best do their job. If we do this too mechanically, it can come across as manipulative. But if you're genuinely curious and honor the coachee's knowledge and skills, it should be relatively easy to enter these conversations and help them come up with the best solutions. This is true because (1) given the highly specialized nature of modern business and vast amounts of information, the coachee will often know better than the coach does, and (2) you get far more support when people solve their own problems.

Coaching is NOT letting people fail when they come up with plans you know won't work. Instead, the coach's job is to help the coachee discover shortcomings in their plan through active listening and open questions. You're an active thinking partner, not "the boss." You do NOT have to refrain from all advice-giving. It's how you give advice that matters.

I might say, "I see what you are thinking there. I've been involved in some similar work in the past. Are you open to an observation?"

Now wait. Wait until the coachee consents.

The coachee will almost always say, "Of course, I want to know what you think." With their permission, you'd give just enough advice to get them on the right path. Then, return to talking it through, holding them as the wisest person in their course of action.

This doesn't mean you don't set standards or hold people accountable. You do. But you don't dictate the exact solutions and changes (barring exceptions for rote tasks and inexperienced employees). In this paradigm of coaching over "training," you go from telling people how to do things to helping them discover things for themselves, become motivated, and play with their learning until they become masters.

In formal coaching circles, there's an expression: Go Slow in Order to Go Fast! Take more time upfront when you coach people. Be patient. Make space for discovery, even when you might know it would be more effective to tell someone how to do something, or faster to do it yourself. Coaching is an investment. It creates great employees who have mastered their jobs. Loyalty and commitment are the return on investment from people who feel supported and appreciated.

Training leaders in formal coaching methodologies is a worthwhile endeavor. A coaching culture can become the dominant leadership style with adequate training among a dispersed leadership group. Its contribution to the positivity of a workplace can't be overstated. It requires humility and patience. The evidence from many studies, and my personal experience as a long-time professional coach, is that it drives great results.

The next chapter picks up on the coaching approach and moves to formal performance evaluation.

Reflections:

1) What's the difference between coaching and training?
2) Can you think of a time when you've coached someone who has far more expertise in their subject than you have?
3) In what processes or functional areas of your organization can you transition from training to coaching?

Actions:

1)

2)

3)

Chapter 23

Rethinking Performance Evaluation

At sixteen, I learned to ride a motorcycle. I realized an important life lesson in the process: literally you will go where you direct your attention.

To earn my motorcycle license, I had to complete a figure eight within a 30'x30' (9.5 meters squared) box.

Every time I tried the maneuver, I'd put my foot on the ground when in the sharp turn. That wasn't allowed. I tried going faster or slower, changing the angle, and even sitting differently on the bike. Nothing worked.

On the last day, the instructor said, "I bet you're looking at the ground when you put your foot down, right?" He told me to try, even if it felt like I was about to tip over, to not look at the ground. The instructor said to look where I wanted to go, and that's where I'd go.

To my astonishment, it worked! I kept my eyes out in front, even as I felt the need to look down. I handled the turns with ease. The instructor later pointed out that's why in single car accidents and even skiing accidents, the person always hits the one wall, pole, or pillar in sight. It's because they're looking where they don't want to go. So that's exactly where they end up.

In this chapter, my aim is to encourage you to reconsider how you handle performance evaluations within your organization. I advocate an essentialist approach: focus on the critical few rather than the trivial many. In most organizations, performance evaluation processes are based on checking boxes around generic process measures. Often, leaders lose sight of the actual outcomes that these measures are about. Therefore, it's critical to *focus* on what really drives the business forward. In addition, you need to know there are two cautionary principles around performance evaluation. I'll get to them near the end of the chapter.

Organizations often fall victim to focusing on evaluating employees' execution of business processes instead of on how they're driving the big outcomes essential to the organization's vision and culture.

So, where should you focus? This takes us to defining the essential.

A simple illustration from business strategist Greg McKeown nicely represents essentialism.

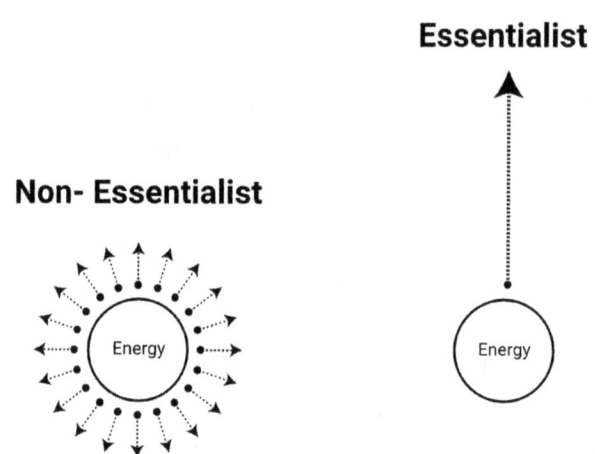

For an organization, this means narrowing key performance indicators (KPIs) to be key performance indicators instead of just PIs. This idea is closely related to the Pareto Principle, popularized by management consultant and author Richard Koch as the 80/20 principle.

This principle is the universal law that most effects/outputs come from a disproportionately small number of causes/inputs. So, 20% of the inputs, activities, and actions lead to 80% of the outputs, results, and effects. For the sake of brevity, I'll skip diving into examples, but you may have some fun googling "Pareto Principle examples."

With most organizations, there are patterns such as over 80% of profit comes from less than 20% of clients, over 80% of profit comes from less than 20% of business units, over 80% of incident reports come from less than 20% of employees, etc. In fact, this ratio is often more like 10% à 90% or 5% à 99% (note the two don't have to sum to 100%).

When we consider performance evaluations, it's critical to focus on the few essential levers we can pull to drive the most important results.

With so many industries, companies, and roles out there, it's difficult to make a sweeping statement that holds true for all businesses, but here are some guiding thoughts.

- Every worker and every team have a role to play. What is that role?
- Each role has associated business processes. Consider whether those processes have metrics that are clearly outcome-oriented.
- What are one or two values most important for that role to embody? Is there an outcome measure that reflects the expression of those values?

A useful exercise can be to list all the business processes associated with a role. First, highlight each one that is, or directly supports, a revenue-generating activity in green. Next, highlight all others in yellow. Now, throw out all things highlighted in yellow. Then, for each item in green, how can you best measure it?

Of course, you should supplement this exercise with big-picture thinking that doesn't overlook the individual contribution to culture, emotional context, and team energy. The thrust of establishing effective performance evaluation is focusing on the essential and measuring it.

We must never let the metric of evaluation eclipse what's being evaluated. When a metric becomes the target outcome, the metric is no longer a good measure.

Rather funny historical accounts of this come from Soviet Russia, where the centralized government compensated manufacturers based on tonnage. So, factories manufactured engines and other machinery that were as heavy as possible. You can imagine a business development analyst, who is assessed, in part, based on the number of leads contacted, recklessly sending out as many emails as possible.

Leaders must establish highly focused performance evaluation metrics that capture the critical few organization-building outcomes while not losing sight of the organizational vision.

The above frames how leaders ought to rethink performance evaluation. In prior chapters, "establishing baseline measures" and "running toward attitude problems," we covered the details of including contributions to culture, emotional context, and workforce energy as explicit parts of employee evaluation.

Here are two final cautionary notes on performance evaluation.

The True Pattern of Performance

When assessing performance for multiple employees, leadership ranks employees or assumes performance fits a bell curve (a la college class grading). Employee performance follows a predictable pattern where a small percentage of employees generate most of the value (that should sound familiar). This is based on research by McKinsey

& Co. Unfortunately, the performance evaluation process at most companies force-fits employees into a bell curve, distorting the true shape of performance, where top workers can outperform average ones by 400% or more.

Therefore, in performance evaluations, focus on identifying both the exceptional over- and under-performers. As McKinsey researchers summarize—many leading companies think "it's a fool's errand to identify and quantify shades of differential performance among the majority of employees, who do a good job but are not among [the outliers]. Identifying clear overperformers and underperformers is important, but conducting annual rating rituals based on the bell curve will not develop the workforce overall. Instead, by getting rid of bureaucratic annual-review processes—and the behavior related to them—companies can focus on getting much higher performance levels out of many more of their employees."[47]

Rising to the Level of Incompetence

Canadian educator, Laurence Peter, developed the concept named after him: the Peter Principle. He wrote that "in a hierarchy, every employee tends to rise to his or her level of incompetence."

Say you work at Twitch and hire Jessica as a software engineer. She excels in technical specifications, project management, and coding. So, she's an exceptional software engineer. After a few years, she progresses to product manager. This is still rather technical, so she does okay. But she struggles with the ambiguity of managing complex products instead of more discrete projects, and she spends almost no time coding. She does well. In a few more years, we promote her to VP. She spends most of her time managing managers and developing client relationships. She struggles.

---

[47] Boris Ewenstein, Bryan Hancock, and Asmus Komm "Ahead of the curve: The future of performance management" in the *McKinsey Quarterly* 2016.

RETHINKING PERFORMANCE EVALUATION

The qualities that made Jessica such a brilliant engineer are the same ones that make her struggle as a VP. We have effectively promoted her into incompetency! The principle of rising to one's level of incompetence recognizes a fundamental flaw in the performance evaluation process—that promotion is usually based on past performance in a role that has little bearing on the new position. They will promote people until they reach a level of incompetence, and they will stay there. Of course, this is disastrous to the effectiveness of an organization.

In evaluating performance, specifically with an eye toward promotion, leaders must consider aligning the employee's skills, experiences, and strengths with the *new* role.

Why are you measuring performance? Does your method identify performance outliers? Does it serve a direct purpose in identifying and cultivating your best people? Does it move the desired workplace culture forward? If the answer isn't a confident "yes," it's time to rethink your evaluation processes.

You've read through the book to this point and hopefully made notes for your action plans in each chapter with its own specified topic. It's now time for a more big-picture, systems perspective.

Reflections:

1) What essential processes or functions generate the vast majority of value within your organization? How do you evaluate performance on these?
2) Are there examples in your organization where you focus too much on the metric itself and not on the thing it is meant to evaluate?
3) Does your organization promote people to their level of incompetence?

4) Does your organization stack and rank employees or look for outlier performers?

Actions:

1)

2)

3)

Chapter 24

A Direct Line to the Ultimate Purpose

I invite you to step back from the usual perspective on business. Most companies are driven by short-term, quantifiable goals (such as quarterly earnings). Unfortunately, this often creates shortsighted motivations that encourage behaviors detrimental to long-term growth and more qualitative progress (such as culture and employee morale).

When you zoom way out, you can view business within the larger economic, social, and even ecological context. The motivation for business arguably is more than maximizing income for corporations (which are nothing more than legal entities) and the individuals within them. In fact, there's plenty of evidence that income, while essential, has its limits for happiness.

Harvard happiness researcher Daniel Gilbert writes that the sentiment that money can't buy happiness is "lovely, popular, and almost certainly wrong." He and others agree that money doesn't buy more happiness but provides an opportunity for happiness where one has greater access to healthcare, leisure time, and autonomy. But he adds, it's "an opportunity that people routinely squander because things they think will make them happy often don't."[48]

Studies by the likes of Daniel Kahneman, a psychology professor at Princeton, show that once we meet basic needs and individuals have a sense of financial security, additional income has only a small impact on happiness. Think of this as diminishing marginal utility

---
[48] Dunn, Gilbert, and Wilson "If Money Doesn't Make You Happy Then You Probably Aren't Spending It Right" in the Journal of Consumer Psychology.

A DIRECT LINE TO THE ULTIMATE PURPOSE

from Economics 101—an extra $500 is a tremendous deal to a college student but trivial to a millionaire. Unfortunately, this distinction is often not recognized.

Today's western cultural values compel us to pursue more happiness from more income—like more money was the end. A paradigm of "more from more," in which one assumes happiness will rise with income forever in a sort of 1:1 linear relationship.

There are limits to what income can bring you, especially when treated as an end. You probably know by now that life's satisfaction depends on far more than money. Humans are compelled to exist in communities: families, neighborhoods, towns, clubs, and cities. And in today's world, you're part of global communities that transcend geographical boundaries. The forces shaping your life and happiness: political, social, environmental, economic, and technological—move in global waves.

When I was a child, connecting with someone from another country—let alone someone on the other side of the world—was pretty much impossible. My kids, on the other hand, grew up playing video games in real-time with people all over the world. They went to college with students who came to Canada to study from every corner of the globe. My youngest presently attends university in France at an international business school.

Even in this global context, people still think of income and economic growth as the most important thing. Yet, when we look at individuals—next door, across the country, and around the world—what everyone really wants is happiness: a sense of well-being, security, and meaning. People want to feel that they are living their lives in a worthwhile way so they may go to bed with a sense of peace and contentment and wake up with a motivation that manifests when their activity is aligned with their most cherished values.

This book advocates for much more than successful workplace HR policies and organizational strategy. It's challenged you to go beyond productivity and profitability. It improves satisfaction both inside and outside workplaces. There's so much cynicism in society today. It's rampant in large organizations where workers are selling their labor to what's seen as an institutional machine. They don't align their hearts and ambitions with their work.

Yet there's a fine line between cynicism and skepticism. Cynicism is a debilitating doubt and contempt for creativity. It's negative, stifling, and lethal to any sense of loyalty to a business. Organizations can become habitually cynical regarding culture.

Skepticism, on the other hand, is a clear-minded inquiry. It demands proof, thorough research, and deep thinking.

So, a book about happiness at work could make you cynical: to think such a goal is blind optimism, a dream, or unicorns and rainbows. But as a skeptical reader, you'd ask, "is there something to this?" Is there science that says you should prioritize positive workplace cultures? This book laid out that science. With this in mind, I believe that the skeptical reader should be convinced that there are substantial economic benefits and benefits to life satisfaction to be derived from the practices described herein.

What if, while maintaining a healthy degree of skepticism, your organization's leaders stepped away from quarterly earnings and business plans and ask, "what's the purpose of being in business?"

Is it not to increase life satisfaction and happiness? Isn't that why you produce the things you produce and do the things you do? To somehow help humanity, not just your customers and clients. But your workforce, communities, and ourselves.

If your organization doesn't contribute this way, you might ask, are you really in the right business? Should you even be in business?

When business focuses on serving a higher purpose, not only will the workforce intrinsically be on board with the company's vision, but the company's long-term economic success is much more likely.

A DIRECT LINE TO THE ULTIMATE PURPOSE

Truly successful organizations—**successful on all levels**—must connect their activity with a vaster vision. This vision includes happiness for employees, investors, leaders, and the world...

Reflections:

1) What are my deepest motivations for contributing to work? My company? The globe?
2) In what ways can I draw a direct line from my business' outputs to increased happiness (less suffering)?
3) Is my work aligned with cultivating greater personal happiness and well-being for myself and others?

Actions:

1)

2)

3)

Conclusion

Beyond Profit and Productivity:
A Happier World

This book laid out the business case for happiness. What follows is a short recap.

First, a short list of benefits of applied positive psychology in the workplace.[49]

- Positive organizational development and change lead to
    o Higher future success expectancy, better coping with stress, and improved job performance and job satisfaction
    o Increase in stock price, better customer and employee relations, and enhanced product quality
- Organizational virtuousness leads to
    o Better organizational performance, higher profit margin, more innovation, higher customer retention, lower employee turnover, and greater quality
- Authentic leadership leads to
    o Higher organizational commitment, organizational performance, job satisfaction, and individual job performance

---

[49] See Donaldson, Mike, & Nakamura's *Positive Psychological Science* 2020.

- Gratitude leads to
    - Decreases in emotional exhaustion
    - More job satisfaction
- Flow leads to
    - Better in-role and extra-role job performance

Modern science confirms that individual happiness leads to success and that this effect "trickles up" to entire organizations. In short, organizations that embrace positive leadership principles and invest in fostering flourishing are more effective than those that don't.

We observed how an organization's culture is felt through emotional context and that the key point of leverage for shaping culture is through frontline supervisors and managers. It's critical to cultivate a sense of organizational citizenship among these workers. If we don't, then bureaucracy and process dictate. If we do, then creativity, self-management, and high performance emerge.

We explained that organizational psychology can be viewed through the lens of Maslow's hierarchy of needs (depicted as a building with layers of related motivations). An organization is the collective expression of employee actualization. To have healthy people and thus a healthy organization, we must nurture a culture in which we meet all needs: physical needs, security, belonging, self-esteem, and self-actualization. Ultimately, when we meet these needs, positive energizers (lightning rods) are created, and the power performance beyond linear cause and effect. They are the magic that creates truly exponential successes.

We then explored the actual implementation and doing of positive organization building. Of the many applications, the essence is that this change should be intentional, strategic, measurable, and genuine. I often say that there are many ways to build a better culture, and only one way not to—to ignore it.

The final offering is a cautionary tale—why the cynical use of happiness tools in the workplace isn't good enough. We need a "***happiness AND***" model.

Let's look at what the thesis of this book is and, just as importantly, what it's not.

A very large environmental protection organization (The Nature Conservancy) famously ran into a lot of trouble in the recent past. That trouble came from poor leadership that entirely ignored the need to create a positive work culture. The results were disastrous.[50]

The non-profit generated top-line revenue of over $1 billion per year. The organization was a very intense, competitive, and efficient operation run primarily by ex-bankers and consultants. At one point, CEO Mark Tercek began an organizational transformation around positivity and mindfulness. He'd been meditating for a long time, using the practice to boost his productivity and performance. Consequently, the organization bought everyone a HeadSpace subscription (a tool to facilitate mindfulness training). The business actively encouraged meditation practice for all employees. They celebrated creating a "mindful organization!" Here's the catch! They had this celebration while employees suffered from overwork, poor communication, and relatively low compensation.

They heralded Mark as a shining example of positive leadership and a champion of workplace happiness while frontline employees and managers were mired in misery. In fact, they praised him for his work in a cover story for Mindful.org.

Then, in 2019, some of the organization's dirty secrets came to light. There were reports that the firm received millions in royalties for allowing oil and gas drilling on protected lands. Allegations also surfaced of years of discrimination, sexual harassment, and cultural abuse. These were directed chiefly toward one of the firm's

---

[50] There are several stories on this. See Zack Coleman's "'The system was broken': How The Nature Conservancy prospered but ran aground" published by Politico.

top-performing presidents, Brian McPeek. Tercek and other key executives covered for McPeek and other abusive leaders. Faced with this growing scandal, McPeek, Tercek, and several other senior officials resigned in 2019.

This is a clear demonstration of what this book *does not* advocate for—and ultimately, what happiness in business *is not*.

The principles in this book aren't a tool for extracting more value out of "human capital," a dehumanizing term commonplace in the corporate vernacular. This book isn't meant to suggest that managers and employees are completely responsible for their own mental health, well-being, and happiness, regardless of absurd or unjust business practices.

An article titled "The Mindfulness Conspiracy," based on the writing of Ronald Purser, points out that mindfulness and the science of happiness have been appropriated and manipulated to justify the abusive excesses of the consumer-capitalist society.[51] In stripping mindfulness, for instance, of its less secular ethical imperatives, it can create a narrative that "happiness is an inside job," and it's up to every individual to accept the circumstances and flourish.

This is like the trend that occurred in environmental activism in the late 70s. Firms like Coca-Cola ran campaigns encouraging individuals to "reduce, reuse, and recycle" and not to be "litterbugs." While this seems great, it diverts attention away from institutional actors and corporate ethics and puts the onus on individuals. As in: "It's not up to large corporations and policymakers to curb consumption or temper extractive environmental practices, rather it's up to Jane and John to do a better job recycling and picking up litter."

Mindfulness, contemplative practice, and the science of happiness, in their commoditized and consumerized forms, postulate that we as individual actors bear the responsibility for functioning in a dysfunctional society, for maintaining sanity in an insane

---

[51] Ronald Purser "The Mindfulness Conspiracy" in the *Guardian*.

socioeconomic environment. This is like telling a plant to flourish without providing sun, soil, and water.

Today's organizational leaders are responsible for the sun, soil, and water for the people they hope to nourish and grow. The larger the organization, the bigger the ethical imperative and subsequent well-being ripple effect. The challenge offered to you then as a reader and leader is what might be called <u>Happiness AND</u>.

This means applying the principles of this book to be happier and more effective AND extending your pursuit of happiness to those around you. Happiness is an inside job AND an outside job. It's up to us to manage stress, contribute positive emotion, and flourish, AND it's up to our institutions and organizations to create a world where these things are possible!

Happiness AND is extending the narrative of the individual to the collective. It's holding the organization accountable in the vaster vision of happiness for the world.

Sure, we can tell our VPs and Senior Managers to reflect, meditate, and facilitate positive communication to be happier. But what do we say to Sarah and Marcus on the frontline? Sarah is a 44-year-old who works two full-time minimum wage jobs—one on the assembly line and one in retail—to pay the bills as she cares for her elderly mother. Marcus is a 32-year-old single father who works sixty hours per week of overnight shift work to put food on the table for his 10-year-old daughter.

What should we, as leaders, say to these folks? Should we get Sarah a free meditation app to better manage the stress of her eighty hours per week of minimum wage work? Should we send a memo about emotional intelligence to Marcus, so he feels less worn out?

What Sarah and Marcus need is *genuine* change. They need organizational leadership that's grounded in a universal happiness ethic. They need leaders like us to take charge and create the necessary change.

A DIRECT LINE TO THE ULTIMATE PURPOSE

It's fitting that this book ends with a call to action. To wake up to the responsibility of humanity that comes with leadership. To wake up to the fact that mindfulness cannot exist without insight into the interdependence of all beings, positive leadership cannot occur without compassionate action for *all stakeholders*, and our happiness cannot flourish without a vision for global well-being.

My wish is that the organizations of today go beyond profit and productivity to a global vision for well-being: to happiness for one and for all.

So, *Beyond Profit and Productivity* isn't a glittering generality or pithy slogan. It's a call to the highest qualities within you. It's a challenge to you as a leader. It's a kick in the ass, a wake-up, and a call to action. I hope you'll take it.

About the Authors

Paul Krismer is the best-selling author of *Whole Person Happiness: How to Be Well in Body, Mind, and Spirit.* He has deep executive experience working for large organizations. Since 2012, he's been an executive coach and consultant to businesses in nearly every sector of the economy. He specializes in the application of positive psychology in leadership and corporate culture.

Paul is a proud member of the International Positive Psychology Association and the Global Federation of Speakers. He's often in the popular press, providing insights into happiness and the absence of happiness in today's workplaces. Past clients include Microsoft, Johnson and Johnson, and both the United States and Canadian militaries.

He works out of his homes in both Las Vegas, Nevada, and Victoria, British Columbia. You can reach him at: Paul@HappinessMeansBusiness.com

Jackson Kerchis believes that the science of happiness has the power to transform the world of business. He combines his experience as a happiness researcher and educator with his business acumen as a management consultant to deliver unique,

ABOUT THE AUTHORS

insightful, and inspiring content at the intersection of happiness and business.

After finishing his economics major at the University of Alabama in two years, he created the world's first Bachelor of Science in Happiness Studies.

Over the next few years, he won research grants, instructed the first Happiness Habits course at the University of Alabama, and lived as a Zen monk.

Since then he has applied his expertise to businesses and military clients. Case studies include: improving safety outcomes for a $600M commercial transport operation, improving emotional intelligence and coaching skillset for national real estate development company, improving wellbeing in the Army National Guard, and executive coaching to the CFO of a major children's hospital.

You can reach Jackson at:
Jackson@HappinessMeansBusiness.com

Find us at www.HappinessMeansBusiness.com

www.ingramcontent.com/pod-product-compliance
Lightning Source LLC
Chambersburg PA
CBHW061603110426
42742CB00039B/2741